THE WAY WE WERE

THE WAY WE WERE

Toni Savage

ISIS
LARGE PRINT
Oxford

First published in Great Britain 2006
by Isis Publishing Ltd.

Published in Large Print 2006 by ISIS Publishing Ltd.,
7 Centremead, Osney Mead, Oxford OX2 0ES
by arrangement with the author

British Library Cataloguing in Publication Data
Savage, Toni
    The way we were. – Large print ed.
    (Isis reminiscence series)
    1. Savage, Toni – Childhood and youth
    2. World War, 1939–1945 – Children
    – Great Britain
    3. World War, 1939–1945
    – Evacuation of civilians – Great Britain
    4. Large type books
    I. Title
    940.5'3161'092

ISBN 0–7531–9344–2 (hb)
ISBN 0–7531–9345–0 (pb)

Printed and bound in Great Britain by
T. J. International Ltd., Padstow, Cornwall

Forty years on when afar and asunder
Parted are those who are singing today,
When we look back and regretfully wonder
What we were like in our work and our play.

Then it may be there will often come o'er you
Glimpses of notes, like the catch of a song,
Visions of childhood will float there before you
Twenty, and thirty, and forty years on.

The school song of Mayfield, Putney, 1944

INTRODUCTION

Growing up is always a battle. It is never easy. The wartime disruption of family life made it harder. Many children were sent off to an alien environment, in conflict with their early experience of the world. "Only" children became part of instant families. The familiar urban enclosed environment was instantly exchanged for one of seemingly endless uninhabited open space. There was no time to lessen the shock.

I write of my experience entirely from memory, for my family were not with me. Children see things solely from their own point of view until they learn to reason. No doubt my playfellows would have remembered some things differently. I invite you into the mind of my childhood. Perhaps it will reawaken for you your own deep memories.

So, here we were. We didn't know each other, which was very strange. Where had we come from? Certainly from the same area of South London, the same school. When a large primary school, having many parallel classes, has to be divided into small units, the new organisation and routine creates instability for a time. We pupils were shuffled like cards in a poker game. Our parents decided whether we should be sent away, or

1

remain. Some sought only the safety of their children. Others had little choice owing to circumstances and some thought that separation, even at such a dangerous time, was undesirable. Thus both pupils and teachers found themselves in new groups. Indeed the youngest infants had hardly settled into school life before everything became strange all over again. For those of us who were taken from our urban roots so dramatically, the experience was quite frightening.

It was September 1st 1939.

CHAPTER
ONE

"We don't want you to go away, but you must. To be safe," someone was saying. "It will be very dangerous here in London. The Germans will go for London because it's the capital. We're only thinking of your safety."

"Why are you staying then?"

"All the children are going. You'll have your school friends. We'll come and see you. Everything will be fine."

It went on and on, this explanation. I couldn't understand it. If it was dangerous, why wasn't Gran, and everyone, coming too. If the Germans came and got them, how would I know. I'd be lost for ever with no-one knowing where or who I was, and my Dad would never find me when he came back from the war. Whatever they said it didn't make sense that I was to be going alone. The suspicion grew. They didn't want me any more. I'd been naughty. Well, why did they give me a Mickey Mouse toothbrush with a whistle on the end if I wasn't meant to blow it, and I didn't mean to frighten Grandad. I just went home with Rita. She took me round all the exciting back alleyways to show me where her Dad worked. There was an awful stink. The smell was ink, she'd said, and the noise was the printing machines. She wasn't going away. I didn't remember that Grandad was meeting me from school, and I'd lost my shoes. I loved my patent leather shoes. I just couldn't remember where they were.

Southfields Station, dismally wet. Red underground train and many children. We all carry boxes and have labels naming us like luggage tied on our coats. Most of us are too miserable to talk, but a few boisterous ones manage to spread fear and bewilderment.

"We're goin' on a boat."

"Nah, we're not, we're goin' to the country. It's miles an' miles away."

"Not ev'ryone's goin'."

"Don't they know it's dangerous, then?"

"It's not dangerous. The war'll be over nex' week."

"How d'you know?"

"The Germans is no good, that's why. We'll just go an' bash 'em up."

"Why are we goin' then?"

I know, but I keep it to myself. We're the ones they don't want, and we're being sent away because we aren't good.

We are all in a big hall, sunny outside and cloudy inside. The hall has a dusty wooden floor which echoes with the sound of noisy feet. At one end is a stage with dark, forbidding curtains. Trestle tables laden with sandwiches, buns, biscuits and beakers of cordial flank the far wall. Ladies, all looking alike in a sort of uniform, urge us to eat. They group and regroup the

4

hordes of children. This herding is eerie. We have lost our identity. I get put here, then there, until a lady, who is sifting through sheaves of paper, says,

"These can go. Four boys and four girls."

We are pushed into a line, counted, and led outside to where a large, dark car is parked. We are all bundled into the back together. The boys claim the pull-down, rear-facing seats excitedly. I doubt if many of us had been in a car before. I had, once, when I was a bridesmaid. People didn't have cars in Southfields. A smallish, lean, weathered man gets into the driving seat and turns to consider his cargo.

"I'm Mr. Raven," he announces firmly, "and I want you all sitting quietly in the back there. It's not far to the house. I work for the lady you're to stay with. Now sit still."

In time we learnt that Mr. Raven was chauffeur, gardener and handyman. He always answered questions simply, but he firmly brooked no nonsense.

"How did you learn to drive?" asked one of the boys admiringly.

"Well, I just got in and taught myself," Mr. Raven told him.

We were impressed. Visions of such a momentous task fired all our imaginations. We compared it to learning to ride a bike, although only one of us admitted to this skill. The conversation ran riot with wild accounts of what might happen should one try to drive a car. Mr. Raven interrupted us dourly.

"Well, you don't take the car out on hills or go fast either. You practise first on a level private bit of road

5

until you get the hang of it. It don't do the engine much good, but 'tisn't dangerous."

By now we were arriving. The car swept along a straight, gravelled drive leading to a large house. The house seemed to grow larger by the second, until the car stopped and Mr. Raven opened the door to let us out. We tumbled out, completely awestruck, to make a frozen tableau, watching as the huge front door opened.

Harrow Hill Copse, as it was named, nestled just below the summit of a long hill which sloped, determinedly, down to the valley at Clandon. It was a country mansion, brick-built, tall, stout and topped with a thick roof of thatch. Shaped rather like a church, the west, north and east wings were square, whilst the south wing was semicircular. This south wing was designed with an open base which made a sunny verandah. Four huge pillars supported the upper floor.

We were standing in the north-west corner with the house towering above us, majestic in its isolation. We didn't know we were at Newlands Corner, famed for its beauty and for the Pilgrims' Way. To us it was another world. My first thought was how strange it was to put dry grass on the roof of a house.

"P'raps it belongs to the King," breathed a quiet voice as we were ushered forward to be welcomed inside.

Mrs. St. Loe Strachey was the most surprising experience of our uniquely surprising day. She was both elderly and vibrant. From my lowliness I saw an incredibly thin, tall figure who stood as straight as a pole. She wore dark, long, thin clothes and held a

6

walking stick as an extension of her arm. Her glasses, gold-wired, were a distance from her eyes. Her skin ruched over the bone like soft calf leather, sculpted into folds. Mrs. Strachey could have been a frightening figure if it were not for her face. The eyes twinkled, her lips twitched at the corners as she studied us. We felt a rapport instantly. We also sensed that this was not someone to cuddle, but someone who would be a friend who knew, and had sympathy with, children. I can now recognise that her keen mind was ageless, that her ideas were modern — even by the standards of today. Undoubtedly she was considered bohemian in her time.

Mrs. Strachey welcomed us warmly, inviting us to sit on the big hall carpet whilst she "explained things". We sat reverently in this entrance area, which seemed so vast as to be as large as a house, and we listened properly. There had been a war before, years ago, when little children like us had lived here for their safety. Now she was pleased to care for us, to share her home, and she hoped we'd be very happy. We were briefly told about the daily organisation and were free to go anywhere outside as long as we could always see the house.

At this point, as Mrs. Strachey turned to speak to someone else, we became aware that two aproned figures were standing in the corner. One was very round and one was very thin.

"These are Miss Bailey and Mrs. Parrot who are going to look after you. Poor little mites. I expect they're hungry. I'll leave you now to have your tea."

By now our energy was replenished. We examined our situation more closely and, as our curiosity seemed to be permitted, we hurtled a barrage of questions at these two friendly faces.

"Is she a friend of the King?"

"Is she very, very rich? She must be a Lady."

"Why's she got a stick?"

"Do you live 'ere wiv 'er?"

We all wanted to know everything, individually, and at once. With gentle patience we were answered whilst being made comfortable. A table, shiny with a bright, yellow-checked covering, stood in the corner by the pantry door. It was circular. It became the hub of our existence, as it had been for the "others", and it radiated a sense of well-being — of continuity. We were persuaded to sit around it on little wooden chairs. We gobbled whilst continuing our inquisition. Lean Mrs. Parrot, the maid, said that she would be looking after us until the governess arrived. Chubby Miss Bailey, the cook, would make our food.

We learned much in those first few days. There was much to learn. None of us went out of sight of the house until we were given permission to do so.

During our stay of over four years there were occasional changes when someone went home, but most of the time we remained an eightsome, for each vacancy was soon filled. That first night there were Valerie, Pat, Joyce, Brian and Peter Stringer, Peter Fitzsimmons, George and me. Brian and Peter were brothers with little more than a year between them. Brian was admirable in his rôle of elder brother. When

8

at last the busy day passed and we realised we were not at home, his comforting arms consoled Peter. Peter Fitzsimmons, Fitz as he was always known, wanted his Mummy. He was inconsolable.

"Mummy. Mummy."

His wail awoke in us all our deprivation. We took up his cry.

"I want my Mummy. I want to go home."

I cried for my Daddy who had gone to be a soldier.

We slept in two enormous rooms. The girls shared the three big beds in the extreme east wing. The boys similarly shared beds in the extreme west wing. Between the two rooms stretched a very long corridor.

So began the new life for Brian who had Peter, Fitz the cry baby, George too little to understand, Valerie the dreamer, Pat called Bun, Joyce-Joan known incomprehensibly as Goosegog at first, but later changed to Goody, and me, Cab. That hurt: Ann Savage — Cabbage — Cab. The more violently one protests, the more relentless grows the opposition; tears; temper; resignation; me, Cab.

CHAPTER
TWO

Our governess arrived. We'd been primed that she had a boy of our age, called Ralph, and that they were German. She was to be called Mrs. Samuel. We were to be very kind and helpful for Mrs. Samuel was very sad about the war.

In truth, Mrs. Samuel was an exceptional woman. The way in which she handled our well-being was exactly right, although we didn't see it that way at the time. Now I recall things which strengthen my admiration for her. I feel sympathy, now that I understand, for the terrible sorrow she must have suffered as a Jewess. The implications of this were meaningless to us then. We often hated her for making us do things we didn't want to do. In consequence we sometimes alienated Ralph.

Ralph was tall, beautifully proportioned and handsome. He had almost black, curly hair, looked older than us and wore a studious expression which matched his serious, studious manner. He was bright. He spoke without any hint of an accent, a fact we found mildly surprising. His minus attributes were that he had his mother here, he tattled to his mother and he was German. When Ralph arrived, George left.

Brian and Peter were unmistakable as brothers. Both fair with bright blue eyes, round-faced and chunky; Peter was a slightly mini-Brian. There was one difference. Brian had a stoicism very like his father's, whereas Peter was less mature with a gleaming spark of devilment. Fitz was ash blond, with an air of determination in his bearing. Women would consider him a pretty boy. Once he settled down, although easily upset, his trait was to be an inspector of things, a "finder".

Goody was a daredevil. Smallish, leanly muscular, she always seemed to be upside down. She hung from anything horizontal, did handstands, climbed like a monkey and would attempt feats which even the boys ruled out. Short brown hair framed her little elfin face. She held her head birdlike, alert, curious, with her brown eyes always questioning.

Valerie, taller and fair, was a dreamer, self-contained; whilst Pat Bun was dark and rotund with the ability to see the funny side of life. Valerie, for an unknown reason, sometimes went away to be replaced by another Joan. Joan Runciman, nicknamed Runci.

Runci, a slightly bigger version of Bun, was naturally motherly. She owned many dolls which were her family of whom she never tired. You found solace with Runci when the activity of the others became wearing or you fell out with them. Her stay became permanent when Pat Bun was taken home so that, whilst we had changes, six of us formed a basic core — Goody, Runci, Ralph, Brian, Peter and me, Cab.

I was tall with legs too long. Brown-haired, brown-eyed, I wore a slightly uncertain air. Never quite sure of myself, I hid behind a mask of confidence which often gave the wrong impression and got me into trouble. I wanted always to be part of anything going on, yet was secretly unsure that I could meet the requirements of the day. My advantage, and often downfall, was that I thought up ideas, however zany, whenever any plans were about to become aborted through lack of resources. I was a natural Heath Robinson. It's very strange, for I can now recognise that I have spent a lifetime of extemporizing solutions which have varied in success.

Mrs. Parrot relinquished, probably with relief, her brief spell of having to cope with us all upon the arrival of our governess. Housekeeping was Mrs. Parrot's trade. Her daughter-in-law was Mrs. Strachey's personal maid. This Mrs. Parrot the younger took charge of us when Mrs. Samuel had a day off. She had a daughter, Peggy, who was about thirteen years old and the three of them lived in a cottage half way down the hill. To us, Peggy and Snow White were synonymous. She was our constant playmate during school holidays when we expected her to devise things for us to do. We all adored her. Her mother was a child's joy: cuddly, loving, understanding and fun. Our bath-nights under her charge were a treasured delight. We girls bathed together in the copious bath. She would allow us to linger in the steamy warmth, singing whilst soaping us, making the ritual a treat. Mrs. Parrot had a strong, mellow voice,

> Hallelujah I'm a bum,
> Hallelujah bum again . . .

"Oo, you said a naughty word."

"No, I didn't. 'Hallelujah give me . . .' "

"But you mustn't say that." Bun was deeply shocked.

"What mustn't I say?"

"YOU know . . . b-u-m."

"Why ever not? Do you know what it means? It's an American word for a tramp, a hobo. They call them bums."

"Oo, but it is a naughty word." She patted herself on the bottom. "You know, here."

"Don't you be a silly. That's your bottom, and it's not naughty. You couldn't sit down without one. 'Hallelujah I'm a bum . . . '."

Undoubtedly, Mrs. Samuel, who coped with us so well, was a wonderful person, although Ralph was the only one to think so at the time. We were told that she had certificates to prove her expertise in physical fitness training. Certainly we had no doubt that she had a bee in her bonnet about it. We had to do daily exercises. We walked bare-footed. We walked shod. With the exception of schooling, feeding, and those occasional days with a much preferred Mrs. Parrot, Mrs. Samuel had sole charge of our care, social training and education in its broadest sense. She was constantly telling us how very lucky we were, and by her lights that was true. She would reiterate that we would look back, when we were grown up, and realise that our childhood spent in the country was an opportunity, an experience, for which we would be eternally grateful. We did not agree. We wanted to go home, but she was right.

Outside, the house was three-quarters bounded by wide, gravel pathways. Opposite the verandah, nestling into the steep hillside, was the horseshoe. This was a level, horseshoe-shaped lawn cut into the hill which rose up from the south side. A wide, curved ornamental wall, rising to about three feet at the deepest point, held back the earth. Lavender bushes planted around the top of the wall provided privacy and shelter. Mrs. Samuel gathered us together on the verandah.

"Now, everyone take off their shoes and socks. We are going to walk barefoot."

"I mustn't take off my shoes."

"Why not, Ann?"

"Granny said so."

"Of course you may take them off. It will make your feet strong and healthy."

"No. I'm goin' to be a lady, and ladies don't take off their shoes. My feet will get big," I protest.

"Cab's goin' ter be a lady, Cab's goin' ter be a lady."

Brian begins the mocking chant and the world seems to join in. Sudden howls of abject misery begin somewhere behind me. I am saved by Goody's sobs.

"I can't take my boots off. I've got weak ankles. My Dad said I'm not allowed to take them off."

Her father always made her wear long buttoned boots, much to her perpetual disgust and frustration. These boots required a tool which was a rod of metal with a shoehorn on one end, and a hook on the other. It wasn't easy to get each hook over its button.

14

Nevertheless, the opportunity to shed them was overridden by the fear of the mysteries of weak ankles. Needless to say, we all eventually had to do battle with the gravel. I seemed to suffer more than anyone else. Goody was soon running about as if she was on softest thistledown. It took me ages to teeter to the safety of the horseshoe.

"Arms up. Arms out," ordered Mrs. Samuel as she stood, facing us, showing us what to do. These became our regular, physical exercise sessions which I secretly enjoyed, but beefed about on principle. I was also a moaner. The activity served only as a warm-up. Long after we would be chasing around the hillside or jumping on and off the wall. A momentary rest is all a child needs to recuperate.

Children exist within a totally different time scale, it seems. In one moment, lying face down in the soft, sweet-smelling grass, a child sees as much as most adults would in an afternoon. I think the speed of growth and learning in early childhood heightens assimilation and sense awareness of all things. Worms, ants, beetles, butterflies and all small creatures were known. Hedges, woods and meadows were viewed as though seen through a magnifying glass. Never again do we automatically see with such clarity and speed. We didn't always seek out things of interest. We could not avoid finding them.

"I've got a grasshopper."

"Where, Fitz?"

"Look here. Aw, it's gorn and left its leg in my fingers."

"You pulled it off."

"No, I never. It jumped away as I was holding it by the leg an' it tore it off itself."

"How can it manage with only one leg?" Goody asks.

"It'll be all right."

"No, it won't. It'll die."

"It'd've died anyway when a bird got it."

I follow Goody down to the wall of the house. She throws her hands down and her legs go up.

"What are you doin'?"

"I'm doin' handstands. I like doin' handstands. Everything is different upside down. You should have a go. Come on. You see what it's like."

I look down her nose and tell her, "I couldn't do it. I think my arms is too thin or my legs is too long. Anyway, I can't do em."

"'Course you can." Goody turns the right way up again. "Everybody can. I'll teach you. Put your hands down there. Right. Now when you jump your legs, I'll catch them and put them on the wall." She views my expression. "Come on. I promise I won't let go, and I'll put you down again."

Several tries later,

"I can't."

"Yes, you can. We nearly did it that time."

This time, my feet are put against the wall by a triumphant Goody, who then lets go so as to lean down and point out the advantages of being upside down. My arms jack-knife. My face scrapes the wall and I hurt. I run to find Miss Bailey.

16

Miss Bailey is an expert cook. Her kitchen is her domain which we are honoured to be allowed in, on occasion, although we were allowed to seek her out in her parlour next to the kitchen. She was just about the roundest, kindest person I've ever met. Always wearing a crisply starched white apron smoothed around her ample frame, it magnified her big smiley face and huge, plump, cuddly arms. Her tummy creaked, like a door that needs oiling, when you were lucky enough to be enveloped in her loving hug. Because she was always there and showed pleasure when we sought her company, we went to her for conversation. I don't think we often abused her tolerance, for if she was busy she would explain why, before firmly shooing us away.

I need her now. Only she can ease my hurt, and smarting indignation, with love and cuddles.

"I want to go home," I sob.

"There, there, my pet. You'll soon feel better," she soothed as she held me close. "Your Gran is coming to see you soon. Mustn't let her see you all upset. She's got enough to worry about with the war an' all. Let's dry those eyes and tidy you up a bit."

Until the war my family had lived, crowded together, in the upstairs of a terraced house, which backed onto a railway in Southfields. Most streets in Southfields were lined with "lookalike" terraced houses. Many were owned by landlords who let them out as two flats, although they made few alterations. Both sets of tenants used the same front door. The lower ones just went through the hallway, whilst the upper tenants just climbed the stairs. The back bedroom was cursorily fitted out to be a kitchen. It had one stone sink with a cold tap, a wooden draining board, a gas stove and a small cupboard for use as a larder. Downstairs had a fire with a back boiler. Their hot water tank was in the upstairs airing cupboard. Upstairs only had hot water in the bathroom which was fitted with a copper geyser. This left three rooms. The front bedroom, used as a living room with a sofa bed, and the big bedroom had coal fires. The little box room over the staircase served as another bedroom.

When my grandfather's business collapsed so did his health, and times were very hard for them. Grandad earned a pittance rent-collecting for the local landlord. I remember his wonderful face. His clear blue eyes twinkled beneath thick, snowy-white brows. His beard and moustache were of Father Christmas proportions. He had been my playmate. Grandad knew many magic tricks. He owned a little box containing a sliding drawer which pulled out from either end. Inside the drawer were three coloured counters set into a tray of green baize. Each time the drawer was pulled out, the counters had changed colour or position. It never failed to fascinate me. Grandad could also draw very skilfully. We would play pencil-and-paper games for hours. He sharpened our pencils with an exceedingly sharp penknife. With the lead resting on his left thumb he pared the wood down to the lead, turning the pencil after each cut, to produce a perfect point. Each time the knife reached his blackening thumb, I marvelled how it was that he didn't cut himself. Grandad was also badly deformed. He had a hump which made his head bow so low, his chin rested on his chest. It made him seem very, very old.

Granny went out to work, which made her seem younger than Grandad, though both were in their middle fifties. She explained her job as looking after all her "ladies" in a big London insurance company. She had a small, blue, hard case which she took with her each day. It always contained a fresh, stiffly starched white apron. On Friday nights it always held some sweets for me.

My unmarried aunt also worked in the City with a Greek shipping company. She would get me ready for school before she left for work each morning. Daddy was already in the Territorial Army. He was weekends, walks in the park, and my whole world.

Granny had arrived.

"Why can't I come home now, Granny?"

"It still isn't safe. We've all had to move out of London now. There's only your Grandfather left at home."

"Why?"

"Because of the war, Silly."

"Why isn't it safe?"

"Well, in London the big buildings might get bombed."

"But what about Grandad?"

"He'll be all right. Don't you worry about that. If there is an air raid, he'll go to the shelter."

I only understand vaguely what she is talking about. I do realise that I don't seem to have a home to go home to now. At least, not until after the war.

(In fact Grandad never went to the shelter, but insisted the safest place to be was to sit behind the living room door which was left ajar. When a landmine was dropped outside on the railway, the ARP warden found him sitting there unscathed in an otherwise destroyed house!

The landlord supplied a virtually identical flat in a nearby street.)

CHAPTER
THREE

In later years, many older people will say that the summers of their childhood were long and gloriously hot. I think it is because we all spent so much of our time outside in those days. Our abundant energy kept us naturally warm. Everything had two alternatives for us. The season was either summer or winter. The days were either good or bad. There was out or in. Out was most of the time. In was something to be endured until we could get out again. Rain was the worst weather for us.

During the holidays and at weekends we had each other. Sometimes we all played together, sometimes in groups. We were a family. At school we seemed to avoid each other. We chose, or were chosen, to be friends with different children. Because we were living so far away from everyone else, school and home were two separate experiences.

On that autumn day when we found ourselves labelled and up for selection, it was still very summery despite the autumn term having begun. We walked to and from school each day. It was about three miles. We had to carry our "boxes". They contained our gas masks. The boxes became increasingly irksome to carry.

As the days passed, and as our confidence grew, so our progress became more active. The boxes were of thick cardboard, exact cuboids, fitted with a long cord knotted into either side. Designed to hang from the shoulder, where the cord cut in uncomfortably, they bounced and banged on our legs or bottoms until we couldn't bear it. We tried out various ways of carrying them and found the knapsack position best with the box on our backs. It was still very uncomfortable and it wasn't surprising that the boxes soon disintegrated, that the cord was for ever pulling out, and that once the rains set in the whole idea was hopeless. A supply of new cardboard nets was kept in the cellar. We must have used many more than someone had thought would be enough.

The gas masks themselves survived more satisfactorily. They were never used, but in the early days of the war there was a fear that gas bombs would be dropped on us. The mask would save our lives. Gas mask practices were organised by the school, which were similar to today's fire drill. We had to put our masks on when a bell was rung. The masks were made of black, evil-smelling, rubber. They had a snout of metal which was heavy and pulled your head down, a rounded rectangular plastic window to look through and buckled straps to be tightened around the head. Having them tested was most unpleasant. We put them on gingerly, trying not to breathe. When capitulation became inevitable, the smell seemed worse each time. The windows fogged over almost immediately. Someone would come to test the fit. This would entail tightening up the straps, which pulled out a lot of hair in the process, plus fingers being pushed between mask and cheek to test that no air could get in. We were then told to blow. Instant joy. Blowing resulted in wonderfully loud "raspberries". We never had to keep our masks on for long.

The day when we were given replacement masks, because we'd grown, was remarkable only because of the new design. The snout was more squashed in. The eye piece was now two large circular lenses. They were rather frightening when we saw what we looked like. In all other respects they were the same.

We did not carry our gas masks for very long. Maybe the Surrey winter caused a shortage of cardboard or, more likely because we were safer in the middle of the countryside, they were left to hang on our pegs at school. We were free.

School, at first, was the cornerstone of our lives. It supplied a continuity in the confusion. It eased the sense of isolation in those first weeks when we were learning to cope with an alien way of life. It provided a routine, an order, which was the only familiar experience left for us. It was my school, although I seemed to know hardly any of the children. Miss Jones the Headmistress was there. So too were Miss Moss and Miss Hall, our teachers. I felt very unsure. No-one explained why so many of the children had stayed in London. A very large primary school whittled down to a very little one made it possible to know everyone quite quickly.

In London, the school had been a proper one. There were three entrances with words carved into the stonework over the arches. BOYS, GIRLS, INFANTS. The large asphalt playground around the building was also divided. The boys were not allowed to play with the girls. To an infant, the Morning Assembly was an awesome experience. On Mondays birthdays were celebrated. Anyone with a birthday during the week was lifted up onto the stage at the end of the hall. Miss Jones invited each child to choose a ribbon rosette from a bag filled with rosettes of all colours. She then pinned the chosen ribbon onto them before leading the singing of the birthday song. Each day we took a penny to school to pay for a bottle of milk at both morning and afternoon break times. We soon discovered that if you only bought one bottle on two days of the week, you'd have four farthings to buy sweets with after school. A farthing was a quarter of a penny. Outside, in the road, there was a man with a barrow. The barrow had a red and white striped canopy like a roof. On the barrow piles of sweets were laid out to tempt us. There were bootlaces of black and red liquorice, sherbet dabs, gobstoppers and sweets in all kinds of shapes, made of toffee, chocolate or liquorice. He came on four afternoons a week, so one farthing would buy sweets on each of those days. You got quite a lot for a farthing.

It wasn't my birthday. I wouldn't be six until after we had gone to Guildford, but I was very unhappy. My family had shortened my name to Toni. It was unheard of then. I suffered endless teasing.

"Tony is a boy's name. She's got a boy's name."

Miss Jones took the problem in hand instantly my misery was noticed. I was allowed to choose a ribbon, and, in front of the whole school, it was ordered that I would be called Ann. It was celebrated as the birth of a new name. No such luck over Cab.

Now urban Saint Michael and All Angels had become a rural oddity in a country house. It didn't seem right to go to school in a house or for it to be bombarded with a horde of noisy children. Cook's Place, as it was called, was the Vicarage which faced the front of Albury Church. Because we were not allowed at the front of the building, I don't think we knew it was a Vicarage or that we should be grateful to the Vicar for his generosity in lending us his home. The pathway we used to the house branched off from the imposing avenue which led up to the church door. This path curved through a dense shrubbery before arriving at the side of a beautiful garden which was landscaped around two sides of the house.

There were no curtains at the windows and the floorboards were bare. Desks had been set in rows in three classrooms. The top juniors had the best room, facing south, with French doors opening onto a long gazebo covered by a rampant wisteria. Miss Hall took this class. It was the universal aim to be in her class. She was a large woman of middle age. Slightly greying, she appeared to be about the same age as all the other grown-ups we knew. Young children don't evaluate age, but they know who they like. Miss Hall talked to you sensibly. She cared about everyone, and this, coupled with her knowledge and the way she taught, drew us to her like a magnet. She would sit outside on the gazebo at break times, ready to meet our questions or to encourage our thoughts.

At first Mrs. Samuel walked the eight of us to school in the morning and met us to walk us home at night. Later we did the journey on our own. There was a bus, a green, single-decker which ran from Guildford to Dorking. We could have caught it at Newlands Corner and got off the stop before Shere, but eight fares were a lot of money, so we walked. We were orderly to begin with. We climbed up the slope of the hill behind the house, past the Ravens' cottage, beside Mr. Raven's huge garden, alongside Plover's Field and down the wild slopes bordering the Shere road. In really bad weather we walked down the road for the rest of the way. Mostly we crossed over the road and travelled cross-country until we reached a farm gate opposite the church. The greatest hazard we faced was stepping in, or being pushed into, the giant cowpats which awaited the unwary. It was rare to see a vehicle of any kind. We never met any people. The return was much more tiring, uphill all the way. We were often puffed out, hot and grumpy until we could see our thatched roof which immediately reminded us it was teatime.

School is loved more than hated because it supplies something to do, somewhere to go. It releases the child from the problem of "what can I do now?" Most early memories are not of how, or what, one was taught. Most are about the good and bad relationships. There was a noticeable sex discrimination in our school activities. The girls skipped, played hopscotch, bowled hoops or spun tops if feeling energetic. They gathered in close friendship groups to gossip or play five stones when feeling sociable. The boys were always on the move, whatever they chose to do. Games like marbles, yo-yos, cricket and tag would suddenly become their sole occupation for no apparent reason. Seemingly overnight, the marbles would disappear and they'd all be making peashooters, playing cops and robbers or cowboys and Indians. Interests came and went, but these interrupted, only for brief spells, their main preoccupation with war games. Whether being aeroplanes or soldiers, we were ignored as they tore around emulating dive bombers, tanks or machine guns. The day they learnt about torture turned their attention to available victims.

"Come on, Cab, we're taking you prisoner."

Not too alarmed, I squawked in the expected way as I was dragged off to a tree in the copse.

"What do we do now?" a boy asked the ringleader.

"We tie her up to the tree."

"Yeah, then we can do the Chinese torture."

"What's torture?" I demand to know.

"Well, it's what they do in the war to make you talk. They do lots of things you can't stand so's you have ter tell. Like dripping water on your head, slowly, for hours, until it bores a hole right into your brains."

"You can't do that to me!" I protest loudly.

A boy named Arthur, who always incites the "let's chase the girls with this big spider" game, leers at me.

"No. But we can do the burnin' straw torture."

Now I feel fear rising.

"What's that?"

"We push a bit of straw down each of your fingernails, see. An' then we light the straws. When they start to burn your fingers, you'll tell us all the secrets."

"I haven't any secrets. Honest. I'll tell — no, I won't. Let me go an' I won't tell Miss," but I'm saved by the bell.

At Harrow Hill Copse it's different. We mix more than at school where, indeed, we rarely acknowledge each other. We have to live together and we have to be together when the weather forces us to stay indoors in the playroom.

Goody is a tomboy. She is accepted by the boys as one of them because her agility and fearlessness are useful to them. She will climb to get birds' eggs from nests which they dare not reach. They take her with them when they go exploring, scrumping and building camps.

"Why can't I come too, Goody?"

"Because you're no good at climbing and things."

"Well, I could still come. I'd be okay."

Goody considers this, for we have become firm friends.

"I'll tell you what. I'll teach you to climb trees," she offers.

"Oo, will you? Then I can come."

"Yes, but not now. I'll teach you tomorrow." She runs away, so I go to find Runci.

"Let's make our own camp Runci. We can make a house, a proper house," I tempt her.

We go down into the woodland below the house and find the right spot. Any good-sized tree with a clear area around it is the place to start. We've learned how to gather just the right hazel branches to build, in wigwam fashion, round the bole. The next job is to thread something in and out of these uprights to fill in the sides. The season determined what was available. Branches of beech leaves or ferns weave well. The result is a private den suitable for any use. In time the woods contained many such dens. They were made for a particular purpose, then were abandoned. We would often discover them with surprise, and reuse them another season. Having made our house, we take our dolls inside. Runci always plays with her dolls. It is her sole pleasure, of which she never tires. We come and go from her company as our need arises, but she, a homebuilder, bears no grudge at our faithlessness. Today I want to play with her because I have a new treasure. For my birthday I was given a black dolly. How I loved her, my Susie. She had dark chocolate-coloured, shiny skin. It felt so smooth to touch. It made me want to be black-skinned too. Gran had knitted a pink dress for her, in basket stitch which I thought so clever and pretty. Runci and I undressed and redressed our babies. We fed them and laid them down to sleep. We went off shopping, content in our rôle play of motherhood. When called for meals, we all responded quickly. We were hungry, and the ritual clean up took time. It was dark when I missed Susie. It was also raining hard. First thing the next morning, Runci and Goody came with me to hunt for Susie. We found her on the steps leading down to the woods. She was sodden, and white. I was horrified. I was inconsolable. That was when Goody offered the climbing lesson.

Woodland spread over the entire hillside below the house, whilst the grassy slopes above became bramble and wild strawberry thickets the further east you went. A well-trodden path divided the two. The oak tree selected by Goody for my lesson grew on the edge of this pathway.

"This is a good tree to learn on," she said knowledgeably. "There's lots of branches to help you up."

I looked at the prospect unenthusiastically, but held my tongue.

"Now, I'll climb up to show you how to do it. You watch me."

She made it look like climbing up outsized stairs. Sitting astride a large horizontal branch, she ordered, "Now you come up." I did try.

"I can't," I wailed. "I can't get up on the first bit." She eyed me scornfully.

"Oh, all right then. I'll come down and help you." She swung down effortlessly. "Right. Put your hand there, your foot there." Issuing authoritative instructions she pushed, pulled, and bullied me up to the branch where she had been. I sat, uncomfortably clinging to the trunk, suddenly aware of my new height.

"Right," said Goody, "that was easy, wasn't it, Cab? Now you know how to do it," and she added dismissively, "you get down the same way."

Monkeylike she climbed down to the ground and smiled up at me. "I said it was easy, didn't I? Come on." She turned to go.

"Don't go. Wait for me," I yelled.

"Well, hurry up then."

I tried, but I couldn't reach the next branch down without sliding off my seat. You need a lissom confidence to launch yourself into space. My muscles were rigid. I clung desperately to the trunk, feeling more insecure by the second. It seemed like hours of screaming later, a very cross Mrs. Samuel stood under my tree.

"Hold my hand," she ordered.

"I can't let go. I can't. I'll fall."

"Nonsense. Give me your hand — just one, then I'll put your foot on the next branch."

It didn't seem as far away as I'd thought. As I descended, under instruction, I realised that I'd been very silly. Climbing wasn't so hard. I could have got down if I'd dared. But my new sense of well-being about trees wasn't enough to sustain me through the punishment. I was sent to our bedroom, and was told that I would not get any tea. I was livid with rage. It wasn't my fault I'd been left up in a tree. Why should I be punished. It was Goody's fault. I did not know that she was also in trouble. Isolated, in ignorance, my anger took control. I ran to the lavatory in the north wing and locked myself in. Self-pity drowns anger. I wept and howled for an eternity.

"Cab. Hey, Cab, open the door." It was our beloved Peggy trying to coax me out.

"No. I'll stay here forever. It's not fair. It wasn't my fault. I'm hungry. I'm goin' to starve to death, then they'll know and be sorry."

A little later Peggy returned.

"Hey, Cab. I've got you a sandwich. Miss Bailey made it for you. Open the door."

"No, I won't."

"Well, lean out of the window then. I'll pass it across to you from the bathroom."

We both leant out of our respective windows. I was petrified I'd fall out, but miraculously reached the proffered sandwich safely. Eating it whilst Peggy soothed with sweet talk calmed me down. So gently bribed, with assurances it would all be forgotten by tomorrow, I capitulated and went to bed.

The only restrictions on outdoor play were torrential rain or blizzard. These imprisoned us in the playroom. We had many things we could do for we all shared the toys in the cupboards. There were lots of bricks, a fort with soldiers, some dolls and teddy bears and jigsaws. We also began to receive toys of our own as presents, so that after a while there was quite a wide choice of playthings. These would keep us amused for a while, until boredom inevitably set in. It was then that play became rowdy and the boys took on a dominant rôle. The girls were made to be "squaws" or "prisoners" and rules were made about the game which you had to obey. One playroom "rule" related to farting. It was the one I truly dreaded. The instant a fart was heard, or smelt, Brian and Ralph forced us to line up with our backs to the cupboard. One person was chosen to be the "detective", and would pass down the row, sniffing everyone in turn until the blame was laid. Total dread, more acute if you were innocent, made you feel yourself blushing to the top of your head as the sniffer drew near. A pandemonium of accusation versus denial usually followed this procedure.

Not surprisingly, the moment the weather improved we were walked. It was when we needed to wear welly boots that we were shown the cellar. At first we left our coats and shoes in our little cloakroom at the rear of the hall. Once winter set in our clothes needed to be dried. Steps led down to the cellar from a doorway opposite the scullery. The cellar was enormous, and smelt mustily of dust and coke. There was one dim light. The open, wooden stairs had a wall down one side and a stout handrail down the other. Once at floor level it took time to become used to the gloom, although the far reaches were always shrouded in deep, dark shadow. We lined up our boots under a long bench against a side wall. Our macs, and any wet clothing, were hung on a row of hooks above. It was very warm. Comfortingly warm. A dusty, black coke stove stood in the centre of the cellar. It was stoked, and serviced, by Mr. Raven. It supplied the hot water, and central heating, for the whole house. The coke lay on the floor, opposite the stairs, in a big, dusty, crunchy, smelly heap. This pile shrank, or grew, as if by magic for we never saw any delivered. A sloping, concrete chute led up to a trap door where the coke came from. Deep in the far end were parcels, boxes, cobwebs and gigantic spiders. In front of this were two, huge, wicker hampers with buckled leather straps. The exit was behind a door opposite the stairs, in the corner. Here concrete steps led up against the northernmost wall. They were safely protected by fencing and shrubs, so that you'd never know they were there at a casual glance.

"There's something in my boot with my foot," squealed Bun as she hopped on one foot, desperately trying to shake off the offending boot.

"Sit on the bench," said Mrs. Samuel firmly. She pulled and Bun's sock came off with the boot. The sock revealed nothing, but the boot, when shaken, released a fat, black, hairy spider. It might just as well have been a tarantula. We girls screamed. Even the boys paled. We all felt as if we too had one in our wellies. No-one ever put their feet into uninspected footwear from that day on.

Eventually, well wrapped-up against the drizzle, we scurried out up the open stairway. Standing there, facing north, it was as if were in the middle of a capital "B". The two bulbous parts of the B were built up lawns curving out above the woods. On the slopes of their edges grew forests of foxgloves and rosebay willowherb which, in their season, decorated the edges of the lawns in a sea of pink flowers. About eight wide stone steps at the centre invited, indeed enticed, you down to the leaf-strewn path into the woods. On our left stretched the gravel driveway, and on our right was the path to my tree. Behind the house, at our backs, lay the hillside with all the choices of routes southward.

"Which way, which way are we going?" we all wanted to know.

"I'll take you to a secret place today," said Mrs. Samuel.

"A secret place," we echoed, "Where? What is it?"

"You'll see when we get there," she answered mysteriously. "Hurry up and don't dawdle. Come on, Fitz, you can hold my hand."

We turned right. We discovered that the wide hillside was rectangular, for when we came to the end of the long pathway, out of sight of the house the path made a sharp right turn. We saw that trees grew all the way round the hillside. At the topmost corner another path led through a tunnel of branches before emerging into a beautifully bright, green meadow. Running, jumping, skipping, seeing and smelling, with all our senses finely tuned, we shouted our pleasure at being somewhere new.

"Just come and look at these spiders," Fitz calls. "They're amazing."

"Come on, Bun," Goody calls, "They're on a web. They can't hurt you. Come on, Cab."

I'm reluctantly drawn to have a look. Webs, woven amongst the brambles, still sparkle with raindrops. The spider under scrutiny is horrific. Its body seems to be puffed up. On the smooth roundness of its black back is a large white cross. It looks as if it might leap at us.

"Ugh," says Bun. "I bet that one's poisonous."

"I bet it would kill you," adds Peter.

"Don't be daft. S'only a blackberry spider. Spiders aren't poisonous here, my Dad told me." Fitz sounds very sure.

"Then why's it got that cross?"

"I think it's to frighten the birds away, so they won't eat them."

"Snakes are poisonous. I bet there's snakes in a place like this," Ralph comments.

The boys start telling each other what they know about snakes. For me, the carefree feeling of the day has sapped away. I walk very warily, alert and watchful. I get admonished for dawdling, until we reach the safety of a beech wood. Now crunchy deep leaves cover our feet. For the joy of making the maximum scrunching noises, we pull our feet through the leaves and kick them up in semicircular waves. Progress is as slow as paddling.

"There," says Mrs. Samuel, "There it is. The biggest tree house you'll ever see."

In front of us, in a clearing, is a beech tree. It is very tall and straight. It branches into an umbrella of orangey leaves high up in the sky. Built completely around the smooth, fat trunk is a wooden house. It has a balcony, supported by thick posts, all the way around it. Wooden steps lead up to this platform.

"Can we go up? Can we go inside and look?"

"No, I'm afraid you can't. It is a private house."

We feel cheated. To have walked so far, and then not to be allowed in.

"Who built it? What children does it belong to? Where are they?"

"Just a minute," laughs Mrs. Samuel, "and I'll tell you all about it. It is not a play house. It is a real house and it's the home of a famous film star named Charles

Laughton. He comes here with his wife when they are on holiday."

"Will he come here soon?" I ask. "Can we ask him if we can see inside?"

"No, I don't think so, Ann. He may not come again until the war is over."

"When the war is over" has become one of those explanations which explain nothing. We run around the tree several times, examining it from every angle, before we lose interest. It seems very odd for grown-ups to live in a tree. Even more puzzling is how they get to it, as there isn't a road anywhere to be seen. As we make our way back I try very hard to imagine all the practicalities involved if you lived in a tree, but I give up because all I have are questions.

CHAPTER
FOUR

I think we all began to wet our beds when we were moved to Guildford. Experts on the subject would not find that surprising under the circumstances. I can remember vividly just how horrible wetting the bed felt. I would be asleep, really cosy and warm, when suddenly I could feel a greater warmth. At the moment when this sensation reached the shoulders, the horrified awareness of what had happened coincided with the urine starting to feel icy cold and the awful smell of it. The only thing to do in the middle of the night was to put on a dressing gown and try to find a dry patch on the edge of the bed. In the morning there were the shame and the gentle recriminations to face. Why hadn't I gone to the lavatory? We were given chamber pots, known as pos or goesunders, which were placed under the bed ready for us to use if we couldn't make it to the lavatory. They didn't cure the problem. Neither did the taunting of the children who had managed to stay dry. Someone must have thought that if we washed our bed things ourselves that might work. This job was done in the bath. In went water, soap and everyone's soiled articles. Often eight little hands were in the bath, pummelling away until the linen was clean: four girls complaining bitterly at having to do this washing because the boys didn't have to do it.

Mrs. Samuel must have spent a lot of time talking the problem over with us individually. I remember that I tried very hard to find out, in myself, what happened. I would lie, wet and miserable, thinking about how it began. When had I wanted to go? When I realised what happened, I couldn't get the explanation out fast enough.

"Mrs. Samuel. Oh Mrs. Samuel. I do get up, and go down to the lavatory 'cos I want to go and I get up and go down the passage and sit on the seat and I go. Only I'm in bed when I've gone."

She took me by the hand and we went to the bedroom.

"Now, Ann," she said, "You get up, or you dream that you do, and you walk down the passage, like this." She led me down to the lavatory. "Sit on the seat," she told me gently. "Now, put your hand down and feel the lavatory bowl. That's right, just under your leg there. What does it feel like."

"It feels cold. Cold and hard."

"Good. Try to remember that. Each time you go, every time you go, put your hand there, where it is now, before you pee. If you do that you won't ever wet the bed again."

"How will this stop me?" I ask, wanting to believe.

"You have to believe me when I tell you that it is not possible to imagine touching anything cold when you are in a nice warm bed. I can understand, Ann, that you

39

can dream you come here, but I know that you won't be able to dream touching something cold and hard."

I faithfully follow her instruction day and night. The next time I dreamed I was on the lavatory, I put my hand down automatically. There was no cold, nothing hard. I woke with a shock. I was still in bed. I leaped out and ran down the passage in both fear and happiness. I was cured. Sometimes I still do it at night when I'm very sleepy.

We asked lots of questions about Mrs. Strachey. There was an aura of mystery about our Mrs. St. Loe. After all she owned our new world. She had a secret, private existence. When we saw her it was special. We learned that she was called Giggy. Everyone called her Giggy. We used her pet name too, but only in private and with a hallowed whisper. When we talked with her we said Mrs. Strachey because it was respectful. Most of the time Giggy was in her library. It was a large room where the walls were bookshelves from floor to ceiling. We thought she had hundreds and thousands of books. She was writing a book. We were warned not to make a noise near her room. We thought she was a very famous person. She often went to London. Mr. Raven drove her there. She was a busy Magistrate, only we didn't know what that was. Sometimes Giggy held dinner parties for very important people. Whenever it was necessary for us to keep quiet, or to keep away from the rooms she was using, we obeyed because we wanted to please her.

The inside of Harrow Hill Copse was fascinating. Even now I can't work out why it was designed so oddly. Upstairs the floor of south side was higher than the north side. But downstairs it was level. As I have said, our bedrooms were at either end of a long passageway. On one side of it, facing south, were the bedrooms for visitors. Right in the middle was the biggest room which curved over the verandah. This was Mrs. Strachey's private apartment. On the other side were several little rooms which all had three steps to go down behind their doors. We were only allowed in one of these, our bathroom and lavatory. In the middle, opposite Giggy's room, was the staircase. Also three steps down, the floor levelled to a landing. To the right, the stairs curved down to the hall. Straight on was Mrs. Samuel's room before a passage turned the corner to lead to the rooms over the north wing where Miss Bailey slept. We did not go in that part of the house, except to use the lavatory there if need be. Under this area was the big hall with our cloakroom at the end and our playroom. Below all this was the cellar.

Our playroom was light and airy. Along one wall was a long cupboard made of a deep red-brown shiny wood. The bottom half was deeper than the top, which gave a small ledge just wide enough to give a foothold when getting something from the top. The doors were not glazed, but had a diamond-patterned wire trellis backed with green silk where the glass would have been. Eight lots of toys, books, paints and games were jammed into the shelves. Four hefty radiators were set under the four wide windowsills. We sat on these, feet a-warming, in the cold weather. The radiators cooled if a lot of hot water was being used, so there were also fireplaces in the main rooms. Ours was set across the far corner and was protected by a metal fireguard. The fires burnt peat, which came in rectangular blocks about thirty centimetres long.

Mrs. Parrott had showed me all the rooms when I had been ill and was off school, but we never broke our bounds uninvited. I held a deep respect for Giggy. I never heard her raise her voice, which was low and slow, nor saw her hurry.

Walking was the occupation favoured by Mrs. Samuel. It kept us out of everyone's way, as well as tiring us out. When we walked, which we did every weekend for seemingly impossible miles, we ran freely over the open country. On lanes or footpaths we crocodiled neatly. You could always avoid the metalled road if you knew how.

For our knowledge of plant, and wildlife, we owed much to Mrs. Samuel. I probably owe her for my large feet and hefty legs as well. We walked to Guildford, to Shere, to Albury, to Merrow and to East Clandon where there was a playground with a gargantuan, rather frightening slide. There could not have been many blades of grass left untrampled by our complaining feet. We walked along the Pilgrims' Way, across the Pilgrims' Way, to places of interest, to the cinema, to school, to swim and to the Post Office. We returned utterly exhausted. We protested that we didn't want to walk, but walk we did and learned something new each time. The visual memories stay with you always.

The route to Albury went down Watery Lane. I thought that the lane must have been a river bed. It was always damp, sometimes very wet, and always slippery. Down, down it went. The overhanging shrubs and trees grew denser and more pendulous until the sky was lost to view. In this natural tunnel the lane was of deeply channelled, opalescent white chalk. Blue stones and black flint gleamed wetly. Should you slip on the clayey streaks in the ruts, only a bath could soak off your plaster coating. So we picked our way with care, ever downwards, certain that we would end up in the bowels of the earth. At a point where Watery Lane took a sharp turn to the left, all our senses became subservient to our sense of smell.

"Cor. Phew. What a pong."

We held our noses and competed, word against word, to express our disgust. Cowsheds stood in a dank row beside the lane. The dung was never dry. Piled high, it steamed silently, the heavy vapour of it hanging in a cloud across our path. The last few metres, to the safety of the road, were a challenge to both balance and lung capacity.

Once in line, along the village pavement, it wasn't far to the centre of the little village of Albury. Here there was a small store. As far as we were concerned it sold sweets and stamps. That's what we came for, usually once a week. Sweets were rationed, as most of the things anyone needed were. Books of coupons were issued by the Government, similar to the child allowance books of today, to make sure that everyone got a fair share of food, clothing and essentials. Children were allowed two ounces of sweets a week. We learnt quickly. The smaller the sweets you chose, the more you got. Dolly mixtures, chocolate drops and jelly babies were favoured. Also, if you tried to make them last whilst the others gobbled theirs up, you would be endlessly pestered to share what you had left. So we ate our sweets pretty quickly and had to wait until our next ration was due. We needed to buy stamps for our letters home.

This day, outside the village hall, a dog darts out into the road just as a van comes along. We hear squealing brakes, a thud and then the calm, authoritarian voice of Mrs. Samuel.

"You are not to look. Look at the wall and keep on walking. There's nothing we can do. Look at the wall. Keep on walking."

We round the next corner. I'd had a swift peep which really only registered a bundle lying in the road. The boys soon help to dispel that innocent image.

"Did you see the blood, Ralph?"

"Yeah, and its guts were all burst out of its side."

"It must've bin dead 'cos the blood was pourin' out all over the road."

They warm to their discussion until they exhaust all possibilities. Now I think that I saw it too and I feel sick.

Westward, along the Pilgrims' Way, there was a steep mount topped by a church. A sandy path, stepped in places, led up to the top. The mount was of sand, like a giant sand dune. It was covered with tussocky grass. It was one of our favourite places because it was such fun to slide down the steep sides. We would climb up the path only to fling ourselves down to the bottom again, where everything we wore would be filled with the soft, white sand. Mrs. Samuel took us there to play occasionally on fine summer afternoons. She had a friend who lived in Merrow, and they would arrange to meet on these excursions. They sat knitting and chatting whilst we were safely, if rowdily, occupied. Mrs. Samuel knitted on one, very long, bendy needle. She also knitted backwards at great speed. It was how knitting was done in her country, she explained. We only became aware of her foreignness with such small revelations. It was forgotten as quickly.

Mrs. Samuel was a middle-sized person. She was neither short nor tall, thin nor fat, yet noticeably very fit. Her hair was black, always worn short, and her eyes were darkest brown. She had a strong face with high cheekbones, firm jaw and a straight nose. Her limbs were muscular. Her skin, tanned and freckled by the sun, heightened the outdoorsy aura she gave off. The clothes she chose were practical and unobtrusive. Skirts with tops, shirt-waisters or, in hot weather, long shorts with sleeveless blouses. The difference between our religious beliefs was something we did not know about. We did have prejudices about race. Or rather, many misconceptions.

What did we know? We knew about Germans. Later we learned there were Japs, who were yellow, slant-eyed and wore funny hats; Yanks, who chewed gum; Indians, who were red and wore feathers; and black people, who lived in Africa in mud huts where missionaries went to teach them to be better. Some of them ate people. Our school books were very Victorian and British Empire biased. We knew that most of the world was coloured pink on the maps, and belonged to the King. Above was a Heaven, which belonged to God.

God was a school subject, although His church was only attended on special days, by the whole school. Christmas and Easter fell in holiday periods, so were of the eggs and trees variety. Three main festivals recurred to consolidate a place in our consciences. The first was to do with sailors and the sea. We gave thanks for the men who faced horrible danger on our behalf. We would have no food at all save for their sailing their ships across the sea for us. There would be no fish to eat if the brave fishermen didn't go down to the sea for us. The sea, black, forbidding and mountainous, tossed the ships around in our minds, with the sailors clinging desperately to the rigging. We sang for God to hear us crying for those in peril, to guard the sailors tossing, and we sang lustily with heartfelt worry.

Harvest Festival came with built-in visual aids. The church seemed cathedral-sized to me. It was an imposingly tall church which made us feel very tiny once we filed into pews. At harvest time it glowed and smelled with the colour and scents of the familiar, exotically presented. Huge floral displays decorated the sides, whilst at the altar golden corn sheaves and baskets of produce equalled the flowers for colour, but with warmer, more mellow tones. Each child had an offering to present in turn. No doubt Mr. Raven supplied ours. Whatever we took up to the Vicar paled into insignificance once at the rail. The sheer abundance of every conceivable fruit and vegetable left mouths agape and noses a-twitch. We always sang "We plough the fields and scatter". We really understood about the snow of winter, the warmth to swell the grain. Breezes, sunshine and rain were our companions. Plough and harvester part of the country. What was a puzzle was why we were giving the stuff back. We'd come to thank God for all his gifts. He grew everything. He could do anything. Why didn't we do something for Him, like some nice pictures for His church, instead of piling all that food at the end of the nave. I suppose someone must have explained it. They didn't succeed

However I did understand all about the Saints. With Saint Michael and All Angels, the third celebration, All Saints Day was second to none. Angels came in different categories. There were those with small wings like swans, white feathered; those with huge, droopy, ostrich-like ones and the ultimate golden-winged. All were neither boy nor girl, but super Holy Beings dressed in flowing, seamless gowns. I learned that we all had a Guardian Angel. Our Angel was always beside us, no matter how naughty we'd been. Our Angel was ever-loving, ever-guarding day and night. Some people saw their Angel if they were very good. Being good made our Angel so happy that we would feel happy too. Saints were all the people who had been good all the time, never doing anything bad, so that God had asked them to sit with Him and keep Him company. Souls were dead people, who with the Saints and Angels made the company of Heaven. Hallelujah. So many happy hymns; so many different alleluias. How we swelled our lungs to pour forth HA HA HA LEY LU JAR!

I also knew all about the golden evening brightening in the west. I saw so many. The evening sun would pour forth a glinting, liquid wash of gold to burnish the fields, the hedges, the trees. Clouds, wispily resembling floating Angels, hovered in the deepening sky. These translucent Angels would blow their golden trumpets to call home the company of Heaven. I knew they would guard the sailors, the soldiers and the souls. For all the Saints, resting from their work, were being blessed in Paradise.

CHAPTER
FIVE

Christmas is coming. The first intimation is the school play in which we all take part. I'm to be a fairy. A nebulous expectancy grows as we rehearse and learn to sing carols. I cannot remember much detail. I have a costume, but when we give our performance it is so bitterly cold that I have to wear it over the top of my clothes. Even I think that it looks ridiculous to be wearing a fairy costume on top of a midnight blue, long-sleeved dress. It dispelled all the magic. I end up in tears. We are all easily upset, having this excitement and expectancy bubbling inside.

There have not been any air-raids, and people begin to think that all the precautions against bomb attacks were just a false alarm. In fact, for the first seven months of the war, life does not change very much in England. So, at Christmas, lots of children are taken home again. (Two thirds of all evacuees went home that first Christmas.)

Valerie and Bun went home for the holidays. The rest of us had to stay. Someone suggests that it would be appreciated if we do a play for Giggy. No doubt it served to keep us occupied until the "big day". It also generated tremendous enthusiasm because of the hampers. The two wicker hampers in the cellar were unbuckled to reveal a delight of wondrous costumes. Not any old dressing-up clothes, they were real children's costumes. Whether we wrote a play to suit the clothes or vice versa didn't matter. Just the pure joy of it all made everything special. Brian was a policeman. Ralph was a jester. Peter was a clown. Goody and Fitz were cat and mouse respectively. Runci was a nurse and I was a proper fairy without a horrible dress to spoil the effect. The show was to be in the verandah room after tea, when it was dark. We were to emerge from the cellar, using that corner of the hall as the wings.

When, finally, the actual moment arrived, it was ethereal. The door to the verandah room was opened to reveal fairyland. A Christmas tree stood in the far corner. It touched the ceiling. The only light came from myriads of little candles twinkling on the tips of its branches. Tinsel garlands hung in deep loops all over the tree, shimmering and sparkling in the candlelight. Because of the wonder of that moment, in later years I always left my own Christmas decorating until Christmas Eve. The expressions on the faces of my own small children showed that they, too, thought it was magic.

As if from a trance, I noticed Giggy with her staff were sitting, smilingly waiting, beside a space cleared for our "stage". We acted our play, which was lovingly received, and then Giggy gave each of us a little gift from the tree. The expectancy and excitement had been fulfilled. We were not given piles of presents. In those days a child might get just one special toy to play with. The toy factories stopped making toys in the war years. Machines were taken over to produce weapons, so it became very difficult to find toys for sale. There was no television, no advertising, so we had no expectations and were not disappointed.

Snowfall could be very deep during our winters in Surrey. There were times when we could not get to school, although we always made an attempt to go.

"Come on, Cab. Get up, or we'll be late."

It is warm in bed, and appallingly cold out of it.

"Come ON, Cab," says Goody. "It's not so bad once you've jumped about a bit."

It's all right for her. She never keeps still long enough to feel the cold. I finally emerge, under duress, because I won't get any breakfast if I don't. Our room, being at the end of the east wing, had three external walls. It was very cold on winter mornings. The wash basin, at the opposite end of the room to my bed, presented an unavoidably chilly journey. This problem was solved when the idea to get dressed inside the bedclothes was tried out. Even better was to pull your clothes into bed to warm them up first. It helped a bit, but once at the basin we had a very quick lick and a promise to pay lip service to hygiene. We knew that our teeth were supposed to be brushed regularly to avoid going to the dentist. Luckily, because we ate so few sweet things, our teeth did not decay. Just as well too, because I avoided cleaning mine whenever I could get away with it. The cleaning stuff was in a round, metal tin box. It was a hard, pink block. You rubbed your wet toothbrush on the surface of the block, which then frothed up to cover the bristles with a foul tasting pink paste. It was like soap. I know because I ate soap once.

Today, thankfully, I have no time left for cleanliness. The effort to get dressed at twice the usual speed warms me up so that I don't even notice the reason for its being so cold. On arrival at the breakfast table the excited chatter about the heavy snowfall in the night supplies the answer.

All our comings and goings will be via the cellar now, and for months to come. Once down there, Valerie, Bun and I think we'd like to stay there. Goody and the boys can't wait to get out into the snow. Mrs. Samuel chivvies us along until, wrapped up and welly-booted, we're ready to set off up the hill. Our breath makes little clouds of white vapour on the bitterly cold air. When we reach the top of the hill our descent becomes impossible. The boys, who are well ahead of the rest of us, shout back, "We've sunk up to our middles, an' it gets deeper!"

"Come back," Mrs. Samuel calls. "We'll try the road instead."

We turn to make the detour to the road, but with the snow topping our boots she capitulates.

"It's no good. We won't be able to get to school whilst the snow is as deep as this. Come on. We will go home."

Whoops of joy greet this decision. What had been an endurance of misery turns into a treat. We throw ourselves down to make body prints in the snow. We select virgin tracts on which to print steps backwards, forwards and sideways. There is so much to be done. After snowballing, there is a giant snowball to be made, which in turn becomes the giant snowman. There are problems of what can be used as a toboggan and where is the best place for a slide.

"When you feel too cold, come in and leave your things to dry out in the cellar," advises Mrs. Samuel.

We spend days in a routine of wrapping up, playing until the cold hits our bones, drying off and then playing indoors. Peggy has a toboggan which she brings up for us all to enjoy. We lurch down the hill on it, two at a time, getting drowned in snow as we fall off and becoming exhausted as we drag it back up the hill. Isn't it really unreasonable that such a pleasurable element can cause so much discomfort. Why can't snow be dry like those small polystyrene beads. One by one, each day, we are drawn by the call of the cellar's warmth. Initially it is lovely, then the thaw begins.

"I'm so cold and so wet," we each complain in turn. It takes ages to deal with our wetness. Inevitably, one day, Goody moans,

"My toes hurt."

"So do mine," says Valerie. "And they itch hurt too."

"Mine hurt as well," I agree. "They look fatter and sort of bluey."

We compare our toes before deciding to show Mrs. Samuel.

"You've got chilblains," she diagnoses. "I will soon make them better for you."

"What's chilblains?" we chorus.

"Well, when your toes, and sometimes your fingers, get very cold, when you warm them up too quickly they go like your toes have. They're called chilblains because they're caused by getting chilled. The worst thing you can do is to warm them up too quickly," she explains. We have all been warming our hands by the stove, and have been sitting on the wide sills of the playroom with our feet on the radiators. I demand, "Well how can we get them warm?"

"People in cold countries rub them with snow."

That sounds too daft to be true, but we're in for a much more unbelievable, unthinkable, course of treatment. Rushed upstairs we are instructed to sit on our pos.

"Why do we have to go on our pos?" asks Valerie. "Why can't we go to the lavatory?"

"Well, you all want to go, don't you?" evades Mrs. Samuel. "You must want to after being out in the cold so long."

We do. In this togetherness, once one goes, we all go.

"Good. Now, you must put one foot in your water. Just the toes will do."

"Ugh. Not in that! Ugh, it smells."

Protest follows protest.

"Your own water is the only thing that will make those toes better," she says very firmly. "When you have soaked one foot for five minutes, you can then soak the other one."

The immediate easing of the pain, plus the sharing of this indignity, earns our acceptance, though not our enthusiasm.

54

There were rumours about the Germans coming. We thought they might be true because, suddenly, we discovered strange objects had appeared. We never saw them being built. Perhaps they were constructed during a holiday period. To us, it was like a miracle. As we crested the hill above the road to Shere, on our way to school, we stopped in amazement.

"Hey. Look at that."

"What are they?"

"They" were a double row of chunky stone pyramids with the tops cut off. They stretched in a line from the other side of the road as far as the eye could see, across the valley. They looked like rows of giant teeth.

"They're tank traps."

"Tank traps?"

"Yeah. Tanks can't get over those. They'd get stuck on 'em. When the Jerries come, they won't be able to move any further an' we'll blow 'em all up."

"But I thought tanks were made for going anywhere."

"Not over them, they can't. Their tracks get caught in the gaps an' they fall over."

"Well, wouldn't they just come up the road or up over this hill, instead?"

The boys stop trying to explain. Mumbling about the stupidity of girls not knowing nothin', they race on. However hard I try to accept that tanks will crash up through the woodlands and meadows to the traps, the more stupid it seems when I'm standing on a perfectly easy hillside above an unprotected road. I know which way I would drive a tank. Halfway down the hill, where we cross the road, we make another discovery. Brian tells us it is a "Pill Box". It is all part of our defence against invasion. This is where the soldiers will guard the road. He glories in his superior knowledge.

"See how thick the concrete is. Really strong that is. The slits is for the guns to poke out of. The soldiers sit inside and can shoot anythin' comin' any way. Come inside. We'll show yer."

The pill box is built high up on a bank hidden by trees and bushes. We go in hesitantly. It is dark inside. As our eyes become accustomed to the gloom, we stumble over the rough, chalk lumped floor to look out of each narrow slit in the walls. I'm astounded by how much you can see of outside. It makes more sense than those tank traps.

We start to play. Running round and round inside and outside. The contrast between inside and outside intensifies as the game evolves into one of defence and attack. Those of us inside realise it is horribly smelly.

"It stinks in ere. Pooh, it really stinks."

"Nah. It's not that bad."

"Yes, it is. I'm not stayin' in ere."

Then Fitz calls, "Look. Someone's done their bisness. Down in this corner. That's why it smells. People 'ave bin doin their bisness in 'ere. Ugh." We pause to look at this atrocity to our defence network with disgust before beating a hasty retreat.

"How're the soldiers goin' to sit in there with that?"

"Aw, they can clean it out, can't they? The floor could do with smoothin' out a bit."

We continue our journey to school. I'm surprised we didn't see the building of these defences, but more than a bit worried that the war seems to be coming, rather than ending.

CHAPTER
SIX

Our families did visit us, albeit infrequently. It was not an easy journey for them. When we had a visitor we were given the use of the parlour. Our relatives were given tea, which must have been very welcome to them, and had the chance to ask about how well we were and how we were behaving. When they had arrived, often unnoticed by us, we were called. Apart from my own family, I can only remember Mr. and Mrs. Stringer with clarity. She was sweet and gentle, and fitted my idea of what a mother should be like. He was a greatly magnified, carbon copy of Brian. The two boys adored, and worried about, him. After one of their visits, Brian and Peter showed us some pebble-like stones which had been taken out of their Dad. They were examined with amazement, and were obviously of comfort to the boys as proof that he was now well again.

Whenever one of us had a visitor, the rest of us would gather on the kitchen steps. Outside the parlour door, which was usually left open, was a tiled porch. We would inch forward onto this porch to draw some of the warmth of the visit to ourselves. As we became known, we too would receive a welcome hug. There were often sweets in the offing. Sweets were such a treat. Families would save up their own sweet coupons so that they could bring a bag of some assortment to be passed around. These extras were especially welcome because the few we bought at the shop in Albury didn't last five minutes.

Conversation wasn't easy with our relatives. We had grown a little apart from one another. We wanted to see them, to be loved by them, but what we really wanted was to go back home with them. Having to sit and talk soon made us fidgety. That was the signal for the watchers to creep right into the parlour and share in the visit. It was my Gran who visited me. She tried to come about once a month, though she found the journey both difficult and exhausting. She was a heavily built woman, and the long climb up from the station at Clandon puffed her out completely. We usually met each other with disapproval. I objected to her lack of enthusiasm at seeing me, and she objected to the state I was in. Most of the time we were all healthily, untidily messy. I could not have shown any sign whatever of being like her idea of how a girl should be. Nevertheless, she undertook the journey, whatever the weather, because she cared for me. Gran still carried her little blue case. She brought whatever she could manage to get to meet the constant demand for replacement clothing. She made everything that she could. As a young woman she had been a dressmaker to Queen Victoria, and was very skilled with her needle.

I learn that Gran is now living with the office staff in the safety of Buckinghamshire. She spends the weekends with Grandad in London and the weekdays in the country. My Aunty Bee is in Windsor because her office has also moved out of London. Daddy, of course, is still living with the Army somewhere. The only other relation I know is Aunty Rene, but she is married and I haven't seen her for a long time.

We all ask when we can go home, but our request is always answered with, "When the war is over." This reply is always joined on to a lecture about how lucky we are and how grateful we should be. It does not console us at all. Goody's Daddy is in London. We talk about our families whenever we are sad.

"My Dad lives in a flat in Hampstead. He goes to work in London."

"Isn't he in the Army, then?"

"No. He's got a very important job, so he has to be in London."

"My Dad is in a camp. Gran said he will come and see me soon."

"My Dad can't come. I have a step-Mummy as well."

"What's a step-Mummy?"

"It's a second one. My Dad got married again. Where's your Mummy, Cab?"

"I haven't got one."

"You must have one. Ev'rybody's got a Mummy."

"Well, I haven't. I've never had one, not ever. Where's your real one, Goody?"

"Oh, she died when I was a baby. I don't like my new one. I love Mrs. Turney best of all. She's lovely. I call her my Mummy. I'd like to go an' live with her for ever an' ever. She lives in Oxshott now with Mr. Turney. He's my other Daddy."

Whenever Goody has been to see Mr. and Mrs. Turney she goes on and on about it until I wish she'd just go to Oxshott and shut up. Then I hope she doesn't.

Of course I had a mother, but I didn't find out until I was about fifteen. It never occurred to me to ask. I found some earrings in a drawer and Gran said they had been my mother's. When I pressed her for details all I got was little bits of information, in dribs and drabs, over a period of time. My mother must have married my Dad after being in love with someone else before she met him. After I was born, she bumped into her previous boyfriend and they must have discovered that they still loved each other. She went off with him. Gran would never forgive her. Dad had been found, walking along the riverbank at night, by a policeman. Dad had been suicidal. For a while he managed me on his own. He put me in a nursery whilst he was at work. Then he joined the Army and I went to live with my grandparents. Gran told me never to mention my mother to Dad because he would be terribly upset. Because I loved him so much, I never did.

There were many subjects which were not talked about in those days. My family kept themselves to themselves. I was not allowed to play out in the street. I used to watch all the other children out of our window, and long to go down and join them. The street was the playground. We never saw a car. Cars were for weddings and funerals. The shops were all small. Everything was sold separately. The grocers sold food, the greengrocer all the fruit and vegetables, the ironmonger all the utensils, and so on. Some things were delivered. The coalman's cart was hauled by two heavy horses. The milkman had a milk-float pulled by a small, frisky horse. There was a family who came round once a week with vegetables piled on a trailer also hauled by a heavy horse. A rag-and-bone man came regularly. He sat up on a cart which was pulled by a very skinny little horse. The man rang a handbell, and shouted "Ragnbones". He'd only stop if anyone ran out with something they wanted to get rid of. In the summer there was an ice-cream man. He rode a bicycle with a big box, similar to a freezer cabinet, in front of the handlebars. Although he only rang his bicycle bell to gain attention, you could always hear him coming because the streets were so quiet. We children always bought his snowfruits. They were ice lollies inside a triangular, cardboard wrapper. I'm sure that they were much tastier than the ice lollies of today.

We all had to sit and write letters to our families regularly. We couldn't think of anything to say. Like most little children's letters, they were brief, and to the point.

Dear Gran
I hope you are well. I am well. Mrs. Samuel says I need some new blue Knickers and my sandals have worn out
Lots of love
Ann

My Dad sent me letters when he could. Soldiers were not allowed to write about what they were doing, so his letters were usually full of questions about me. Suddenly, wonderfully, he was going to come. Dad was the nucleus of my whole being. I had not seen him since I left London. I bragged wildly about him from imagination. It was unknowingly mean, and excessive under the circumstances. The other dads were either excused fighting on health grounds, or were doing essential war work. I drove everyone mad with my chatter. Dad was tall, handsome, brave, smart, important, busy winning the war and any attribute which came to mind was added to my description of him.

When at last I saw him marching up the drive, my make-believe became reality. He swept me up as easily as if I was a bag of feathers and carried me into the parlour. I sat on his knee, holding him and being held. My skin felt too fragile to contain all the love and pride swelling inside me. I knew that this was a precious time, for he was going away to somewhere over the sea. Over the sea had no real meaning, but a long way I understood. Now it was my turn to have a huddle of watchers waiting to join us. Goody was in the front.

"This is my best friend," I say, giving her the chance to come in. Dad lifts her up to sit on his other knee. The little green god of jealousy makes me angry. I push at her.

"It's my Dad. He's mine!"

"This is your best friend," Dad admonishs me. "She has no-one to visit her. I have two knees. Why can't she share a moment? It won't hurt you."

I feel ashamed. Of course he's right. I feel guilty at my selfishness. Just being close, belonging to him, is enough. In the doorway, Brian, Peter and Ralph are edging closer. I can see admiration and approval in their expressions. I feed on my happiness as a bee draws on nectar. The afternoon is golden.

We all wave him goodbye as he strides off to go his long way. My eyes spill my sadness quietly down my cheeks, and drip off my chin.

"He's great, your Dad," says Brian.

"Yeah, great," echo the others.

"I wish I had a Dad like yours," says Goody with a wistful sigh.

"You can always share mine," I offer because she is my friend. "Next time, when he comes back, we'll have half each."

We squeeze each other's hands, and continue with the day.

Of course our visitors supplied many answers to our worries and concerns. We wanted to know that everyone was safe and where they were. I was happy that my family were away from London but worried about Grandad. To us, London was the war.

Late one night, we all knelt on my bed to watch the sky from the north-facing window above my pillow. We were staring at a huge, orangey-red glow shimmering on the horizon. It didn't do anything spectacular, it was just there.

"That's London," said Brian, who always seemed so sure of his information. "It's burnin'. It's on fire."

"Why's it burnin'?"

"It's bin bombed, silly. The bombs catch it on fire."

"Is it all on fire?" I asked, thinking of Grandad.

"A lot of it is," Ralph pointed out. "That must be quite a big fire. But London is a very big place, so it won't be all of it."

We fell silent, each one deep in their imaginings. Was the fire destroying our homes? Could people escape? It was Giggy who came and persuaded us back to our own beds. She spoke softly.

"It is only the middle of London, my dears. Not where your families are."

We lay, each trying to make some sense out of this incompleteness in our minds, until we slept.

It was a year after we'd been evacuated when London was bombed. The Blitz, the regular bombing of the big cities, began on September 7th, 1940.

CHAPTER
SEVEN

Sleep was disturbed sometimes. Not a wide awakening disturbance, but a semi-conscious awareness of noises. The most frequently recurring sound was that made by the convoys. There were nights when it seemed as if lorries were grinding up the hill endlessly. The hillside echoed to the sound of engines battling with the steep gradient. The protesting whine changed pitch with the variation of the slope. One lorry after another reproduced the notes as if from a written score, and the music had no beginning and no end. We always presumed that the convoys were going from Clandon towards Shere. I suppose they could have been travelling the other way, for both sides of the hill were steep.

The conversation at breakfast would prove that we all heard them.

"Did you hear the lorries last night?"

"Yeah. There must've bin hundreds, thousands probably."

"All night they was movin'."

"Where'd you think they was goin'?"

"To the war, of course."

I speculated that perhaps my Dad was in one of those lorries. It was just as well that I did not know the truth then. Dad was in hospital having a metal plate put in his shin bone. He'd been in a bunker in Dover when a direct hit by a bomb flattened the building. He had been buried under rubble which crushed one of his legs.

The other disturbance to sleep were the aeroplanes. The boys said you could easily tell the goodies from the baddies. Peter was good at mimicking the noise they made.

"Go on, Peter," Brian urged his brother. "You show 'em how they can tell the difference."

"Well, our planes just go yeowrrrrr!" Peter roared as, with arms outstretched, he zoomed round the room. "You can't mistake the Jerries. They've got a little stop in their noise. They go yeum-yeum-yeum," he droned.

"Why's their planes different?" we ask, wondering how they know all this.

"They've got different engines, of course. Oh, you are stupid," Brian groans.

I listened when the next infringement of our airspace occurred. Holding my breath, I concentrated on the sound. Still I wasn't sure. The noises seeping into my woolly, sleep-fogged brain all seemed to be the same. Soft, deep bangs in slow succession mix in with the droning. Whump, whump, whump. I sleep.

At the breakfast table the morning after the air is filled with excited chatter.

"Did you hear the bombs?"

"Bombs?"

"They were incendaries."

"What's incendreys?"

"We're goin' out straight after breakfast to find their tails," Fitz announces.

"What's incendreys?"

Brian gives a deep sigh, and then explains,

"Incendaries are bombs. Not big bombs that knock houses down. They're little bombs which set fire to the things they fall on. They burn up quickly, but you can find the fin if you can find where they fell."

"Why did they drop 'em 'ere? Are they tryin' to bomb us?"

"No, stupid. They just throw them out anywhere to get rid of them. They're runnin' away see? Our fighters is too good for the Jerries. They are chasin' 'em away, shootin 'em down so they they throw away their bombs to make their planes lighter," he paused to look at us girls pityingly. Then with quick anticipation he added, "Then they can move quicker, 'cos they're not so heavy any more. See?"

"Can we come with you to find the tails?"

"No. Well, all right then, but we bags all the ones we find."

We couldn't keep up with them as they raced up the hill, through the trees, and spread out over the top field. We caught up with Fitz when he stopped to examine something. He was standing by a circular ash-filled dent in the ground, and was holding an oddly shaped object.

"What you got, Fitz?" we panted.

"It's a tail, an incendary fin."

"Is it hot?"

"No. See, look it's the bit off the end. This ring was around the bit that burned, and these flat bits are to help it whistle as it comes down." He held it out to us. I didn't want to touch it, but Goody took it. We examined it closely. I looked at the ground.

"It didn't burn much, did it?"

"There's nothing to burn here. It's houses and things wot it would catch alight. I'm goin' to look for more. There's a whole row right across," he points vaguely into the distance. We decide to return home again. I want to ask questions about our safety, and check up on the boys' information.

"Now, how would an aeroplane in the dark know that a house was here?" Miss Bailey asked. "Why do you think we make sure that the blackout curtains are all properly closed at night? No. No-one would ever know that a house was here." She gives me a big hug of comfort. "Don't you be worrying, my dear. There's no chance of a bomb hitting us when there's all this open space around us. The Germans are just throwing away their bombs on the fields as they fly back to Germany."

I feel better. One could fall on the house by mistake, I suppose, but they weren't trying to hit us.

These incidents helped us not to panic the night there was a tremendous thump. This time it was a land mine which had fallen in the middle of a field. We went for a walk especially to see where it had landed. Mrs. Samuel led us down the steps to the bottom of the woodland path, where it was crossed by a well-used footpath. Under a canopy of broad-leaved trees, the way left led to Mrs. Parrot's cottage. The way right led down to West Clandon Farm nestling in the valley. We had not been this way before. At the very end, at the forest's edge, was a stile from which you could see the whole valley spread out below. The farm was tucked neatly into a fold of the rolling fields. It was well-protected from all but the southern side. A wide farm track curved round from the farm gate to pass the stile on its way to somewhere. We all trooped down this track to visit the farm and to find out what had happened. On the left hand side was a large, sloping, ready-ploughed field. In the middle of it was a huge white hole. Our breaths whistled out in incredulity.

"Can we go an' have a look?"

"When we've been to see the farmer and his wife. And if he says you may."

Having learned that everyone was unharmed, our patience was overstrained as we waited for the grown-ups to stop their gossiping. We were bursting with curiosity. At last we were given permission to go over the field to see the hole. The whiteness was chalk. Chalk had been blown out of the ground, scattering in decreasing density around the perimeter of the hole. From the distance, this had made it look enormous. Seen from the edge, it was the depth, not the width, which astonished us. It seemed that a lot of good, solid earth had just evaporated. It was unthinkable that a bomb could do that. I pondered on why they called it a land mine when it had been dropped from the air. We had a lot to tell Miss Bailey.

"Now you can see why all of our windows have these paper crosses on them," she said. "Explosions like that make a big blast of air which could break the glass. The gummed paper would stop the panes falling out."

I can understand this, now I have seen the hole.

Beside the path alongside the parlour wall is a kitchen garden. In size it is roughly equal to three allotments. It is surrounded by a thick privet hedge. There is one way in through a wicket gate in the side facing the house. Above this garden the hill rises steeply, and a single wire and post fence stretches from the end of the hedge up to Mr. Raven's gate. There doesn't seem to be any reason for the fence. It simply cuts the hillside in two, though the land does level out behind the wire to a flatter meadow. This meadow, bounded by the gravelled drive and the dirt road leading to the Ravens' house, is the only suitable place to play ball games. In the corner, where the fence meets the privet hedge, it is warm and private. Unless someone is in the horseshoe, you can't be seen there. It is one of those places where you can discuss plans. Goody and I lie in the warm grass, chewing sorrel stalks, and thinking. As always, she doesn't keep still for long. She begins a series of handstands into the resilient hedge.

"Hey, Cab," she exclaims in delight, "this is where you can learn to do this."

"I can't do them. You know I can't," I reply stubbornly.

"Listen. It's okay. The hill slopes down, which will help you get up. The hedge is soft, so you won't get hurt. Come on."

"Oh. All right. I'll have one more try, but if I can't, then I can't."

Under instruction, I throw myself into the effort. Hands down, legs unevenly up, so that one leg always pulls the other one down again. I feel helping hands on my reluctant leg. Both of my calves touch the hedge. All in an instant, as she shouts our success, my long legs press further and further into the privet's twiggy depths until, at an angle of forty-five degrees, I fall on my shoulders with legs entrapped. Whilst I try to get out of the hedge, Goody rolls around in helpless mirth. My legs are extensively scratched. I want to hit her, but a cross male voice shouts at us and makes us freeze.

"'Ere. What are you doing? Leave my hedge alone!"

We look at each other in puzzlement, wondering where the voice is coming from. It seems to be inside the hedge, so we both scurry round to look through the gate.

"Oh, Mr. Raven, it's you!" we exclaim.

"Yes, it's me," he answers, "And you just keep off my hedge. I have trouble enough with the bloomin' rabbits. I've put chicken wire all round the inside and at the bottom of my gate to keep the darn things out. I don't want you makin' holes all over the place lettin' them get in."

"What are you doing?" Our question gives him the opportunity to rest from his hoeing.

"Keeping these weeds down. It takes a lot of veg to keep you lot fed. I grow all the food for the house," he says proudly. "These here are carrots. Over there's my peas, an' they'll soon be ready for pickin'."

"Can we help you?"

"No, thanks. You just keep outa my gardens. The fewer feet trampling about, the better. And make sure you don't damage my hedge. Now be off with you."

Mr. and Mrs. Raven lived in a house on the top of the hill. Their house stood beside the dirt track and had rows of outbuildings behind it. There was a shed for Mrs. Strachey's car, several storage sheds and a large chicken house. Their back gate, in line with the boundary fence, was no deterrent to the chickens. They were free ranging in the broadest sense. They wandered wherever they pleased. Mr. Raven had an enormous garden. It stretched southward to the edge of Plover's Field and was laid in plots divided up by grass pathways. There were also very many fruit trees, and bushes. Each in season tempted us to scrump. There were cherries, plums, gooseberries, pears, strawberries, raspberries and a variety of different apples. Mr. Raven's industriousness must have made Giggy's household completely self-sufficient in greengrocery. Meat was rationed. Each person was only allowed a small portion a week. In the country there were ways of getting extra supplies. Rabbits were trapped, pigeons were shot and, when the hens had finished laying eggs, they also added to the food supply. Although everyone got enough to eat, people who remembered being able to have anything they wanted found it hard to manage with so little. We were aware of their concern about food. The popular songs of the time, learned mostly from Mrs. Parrot, reflected this.

"Ma, I miss your apple pie, Ma, I miss your stew," we all sang loudly, and "Run rabbit, run rabbit, run, run, run," is still sung in school singing lessons today.

Mrs. Raven must have done the washing for the big house. Long clotheslines of wire were attached to poles either side of her back path. These were usually filled with billowing linen in the ever-present breeze. She also looked after the chickens. Miss Bailey would ask us, in turn, to fetch the eggs. Sometimes Mrs. Raven wouldn't have collected them when we arrived, so we were invited to join in the hunt for them. Free-range chickens lay eggs in very funny places which made the task a lot of fun. It wasn't long before we got to know all their hidey holes and were welcomed to help regularly. We were allowed to feed the hens as a reward. Miss Bailey could not have managed without those eggs. The ration, from the shop, was one egg, per person, a week.

We never went hungry but, like all healthy children, we would eat anything extra that came our way. Because no-one forced us to try things, we tried anything edible. It gave us a liking for a great variety of foods. Some of our "extras" grew naturally, like wild strawberries, blackberries, sloes, nuts and crab apples. Some we scrumped, like raspberries, gooseberries, raw maize, carrots, peas, mangelwurzels and fruit from the orchard.

CHAPTER
EIGHT

Everyone acknowledged that Miss Bailey was a fantastic cook. We would beg to be allowed to help in the kitchen. At first we were given the job of shucking peas, which we did sitting outside on the kitchen steps. Later, standing on a chair at the kitchen sink, we were trusted to scrape the new potatoes and young carrots. To be inside was reward enough. It was so warm and cosy. Sometimes we were given a taste of something special Miss Bailey had cooked. If we didn't behave we were sent out and not chosen to help again for a long time.

The kitchen area took up the whole of the east wing. It was sandwiched between the parlour and the scullery. The parlour had the porch in front of it. The scullery had the walk-in larder behind it, but the kitchen took up the whole width of the wing. There were big windows at either end. One gave a view of the horseshoe, the other a view of the driveway. Under this one was an enormous kitchen sink with draining boards and worktops. This was the cook's sink. Through the door on the right in the scullery was another sink. This was for the maid to use to do the washing up and the cleaning. In here was the big hatch opening into the verandah room which was used to pass the food through and to pass the dirty plates back.

Miss Bailey cooked all her wonderful recipes on, or in, a long oil-fired cooker which backed onto the parlour wall. On top were a row of burners. Underneath were two ovens. The bluey flames looked like gas flames, but the smell, much nicer, was warmly oily. Cupboards, tables and chairs completed the kitchen furnishing.

Giggy gave dinner parties. The guests came, dined, and left unseen. The next day there were often tasty left-overs. The outstanding treat was to be given a coffee cream. These delectable little pots of dessert were cooked, and served in their pots. Very coffee tasting, they resembled in texture a cross between junket and egg custard. The "skin-man" was deliciously chewy, the cream melted in the mouth. There was never enough in a pot.

"Why are they so small?" I asked.

"Because the visitors have lots of other things to eat as well. They couldn't manage a bigger one," Miss Bailey explained.

"I could eat a bigger one. I could eat lots," I said, smacking my lips.

"Ah, but they're only meant to be a little taste," she said with a smile. It didn't seem at all logical to me.

Childhood memories of food are usually of those tastes violently hated or particularly enjoyed. I had a real aversion to fat. Stew was a frequent meal which sometimes contained chunks of fat depending on which meat was used. I found it impossible to eat the bits of fat. The taste, to me, was revolting, the sensation of its slimy slither down my throat made me heave. Ralph advised me to hold my nose. It was a well-known trick which usually worked, but even this couldn't alleviate the nausea of swallowing. All the cajoling arguments were useless, as was being left at the table until it was eaten. At times like this we were all very supportive of one another, and felt great sympathy for the person faced with food they disliked. Fat stew was the worst food to me. Oh, but stewed wild strawberries: now that was the food of the gods. There is a truly unforgettable taste in a wild strawberry. How such a little pea-sized berry can have such a delicious taste is miraculous. The strawberries grew amongst the brambles all over the hillside. About mid-June the harvest would appear. Armed with bowls and jars, we would scour every inch of ground to collect a pudding's worth. Each time we gathered only those which were really ripe, eating as we picked, as all fruit pickers do. There were plenty. Once, in mid-field, I found a mutant. It was as large as a cherry. I held it up, triumphantly, for all to marvel at its size.

"Look at this. Look at this gigantic . . ."

"Let's see," interrupted Goody, stepping close.

With a flashing snatch it went from my fingers into her mouth.

"Yum. That was good," she said as she skipped swiftly out of reach. The hill echoed with my shouts of anger and anguish. It wasn't fair.

We took our filled containers to Miss Bailey. What she did with them we didn't know, but the resultant tureen of warm, rosy fruit was eaten with reverence. The wonderful smell of it foretold the taste.

It was the boys who came up with the idea of a cook-out. We'd been building camps of all kinds. It was natural, I suppose, to want to eat in them. We sat and made plans.

"We can get eggs easy," Fitz stated. "There's always some near the fence, out of sight."

"I can get some potatoes. They've just bin dug and are in a heap by the kitchen," Peter offered.

"You'll get caught pinchin' those," warned Valerie.

"No, I won't. Not if I'm careful."

Brian knew he can scrump some peas, and our scheme gathered momentum until Ralph said,

"What are we going to cook it all in?"

It was as if a light had been switched off. The brightness went out of the day.

"We'll never be able to get pots and pans," Ralph added heavily, "Never."

We sat, in deep gloom, mulling over what might have been. I didn't give up easily. I racked my brain. There must be a way.

"I know," I announced enthusiastically, "The dustbin. There's always cans and things in the dustbin. There's those big treacle tins. We can rinse them out and use them."

My idea took hold.

"Yeah, that's okay, Cab. You see what you can find. Everybody get the stuff an' we'll meet at the top camp."

The top camp was deep in the centre of the copse outlining the summit of the hill. The trouble with inspired, and hasty, ideas came when you tried to put them into effect. Rooting about in the dustbin without being seen was a nasty, heart-thumping experience. I managed to grab one sticky golden syrup tin, one smelly old baked bean can and one large fruit tin. Panting with fear, I crouched down behind the cellar steps to recover. Around the corner, between playroom and Giggy's room, towered a water butt. It was the father of all water butts, storing rainwater from all the gutters. Next to the butt, right in the corner, were French windows leading to the hall via our cloakroom. I considered washing the cans in our washbasin. It was too risky. I opted instead to give them a quick swill with rainwater. The butt hid me from Giggy's window. There wasn't anyone in our playroom, so I swung the tap handle, which was set about waist height, and struggled to remove the treacle in a trickle of water.

"You must never touch that tap."

I spun round to see Mrs. Parrot right beside me.

"I only wanted to wash,"

"I can see that," she interrupted sharply. "This is Giggy's water. You must never touch it."

"What's it for, then? Does she drink it?"

"No, you daft ha'porth," she was laughing. "This is pure rainwater. Giggy always washes in rainwater. It keeps her skin and hair beautifully soft. If you all go using it, she won't be at all pleased. Now off you go."

I go. Never would I touch Giggy's butt again. I stealthily make my way up the hill. The boys have already built a fire which, we're informed solemnly, is properly made like the scouts do it. I offer up my cans proudly. Our collective efforts have succeeded in getting all that we needed. The final problem is how to do the cooking, and all we can do is try. The results don't look inviting. The eggs sizzle in a syrupy gunge. The peas stick in the dregs of the baked bean can and the potatoes topple over to fall into the fire.

"Doesn't matter, that doesn't," says Ralph with conviction. "Potatoes can cook just in the fire. They'll be smashing."

We eat the black potatoes, the peculiarly coloured peas, and the hard, crispily sweet, eggs with raw carrot. We dare not admit that the feast is anything other than delicious. Suddenly we are aware that Giggy is standing beside us. There is no escape. We are petrified.

"You will," she speaks very softly, "You will make quite sure that you put out that fire completely when you tidy up." And then she's gone. We are awestruck.

"She didn't tell us off."

"P'raps she didn't mind."

Never was a fire extinguished more thoroughly than ours, or a place left tidier.

Giggy must have been concerned that we should know, and appreciate, what was to be our history. There were about three occasions during our stay when we were summoned to her room at night. They were solemn events. We were led quietly, in our nightclothes, into Giggy's library. In the hushed dimness there was an air of expectancy. It was obviously a deeply serious gathering.

"Sit here, on my little rug," she would say. "We are going to listen to the radio. What you will hear is of tremendous importance. The Prime Minister is about to speak to everyone in the Country."

Her "little rug" was quite a large carpet, so we sat, separate and still, with bated breath as the radio was switched on.

"Bom, Bom, Bom, Bohm; Bom, Bom, Bom, Bohm," boomed the musical drum beats. Then a man was speaking. Slowly, clearly, and with deep solemnity. I remember only the voice. (These masterful speeches by Winston Churchill were often replayed in later years, when we were able to understand, and remember their content.) When he had finished, we were taken, silent and overawed, back to bed.

CHAPTER
NINE

All things new had a spark with a tendency to light an inferno of wild, temporary enthusiasm. The Christmas play started a stage-struck acting phase. The concert made great singers of us all. The *Just So* stories created a new generation of explorers, but, for a visit by the Queen, the enthusiasm was already lit and was permanent. We were Royalists.

Word had got around that our Queen had come. She was visiting her dressmaker. Her dressmaker lived in Albury Manor which was not very far from Cook's Place. The tall, wrought-iron gates of the manor were on the corner of the road leading up to Albury Heath. In answer to our questions, Miss Jones said that we would go to see her. That she would wave to us. We were going to walk down to the junction to stand alongside the road opposite the gates, and wait for the Queen to come by.

"She might stop an' talk to us."

"No. She's much too busy."

"But she might stop, when she sees us all wavin' an' cheerin'."

"She'll be goin 'ome to 'er castle wiv all 'er new robes an' stuff. She won't notice us."

"She can't miss seein' us. We'll be standin' right where she comes out of the gate."

I listened to all the opinions and got an idea.

"Miss, Miss, can we give the Queen some flowers? She might just stop long enough for us to give 'er some flowers."

"That is a nice idea, Ann. Yes, we'll find some and you can hold them. If the Queen's car does stop, you may step forward to present them with a little curtsey."

The Queen is here now. No warning. No planning, just grapevine information. No time to practise a curtsey. We are lined up. Our crocodile, bubbling with excitement, hurries down the road. I'm given a bunch of flowers to hold. I seem to remember they were a few, very lovely, lilies. We all fidget and crane our necks, whilst in my head I imagine what might happen.

"Your Majesty . . ."

"Your Royal Highness . . ."

There's the car. It's coming, it's coming, everyone shouts. The shiny, black limousine purrs past the waving sea of whooping, cheering, bouncing little bodies; and is gone.

"Oh, Miss. She never saw the flowers. She should've stopped for her flowers."

It is like that dead dog all over again. Did I really see the Queen, or did I think I had? I feel very sad, and disappointed.

With the increasing warmth of early summer, the scents and smells of the countryside intensify. Those scents and smells which are experienced in childhood remain, like keys in the doorways of the mind, ready to unlock memories associated with them. Beside the kitchen steps was a lead tank. It was that lovely, sullen, deep, cloud-like grey, and the sides were embossed with a pattern of twisting vines. The inside was planted with nasturtiums, which trailed long tendrils over the edges to glow against the grey. The flowers, from deepest red through orange to palest yellow, had a scent which hung heavily on the air around the steps. Sunshine on the flowers heightened their hot, pungent odour. They smelled like the taste of their seeds. The smell of nasturtiums meant nits.

It was a place, well-chosen by Miss Bailey, for us to suffer the discomfort of the nit comb. Sitting on the steps, we would succumb to the heady warmth and become indolent. Head lice flourished in the war years. The only way to get rid of them was to comb out from the hair all the nits and the eggs. Miss Bailey would sit, legs akimbo, on the lobby floor whilst we would sit, in turns, on the steps between her knees. It was my turn. We talked lazily. The combing and pulling soon became unbearable. It was only the soothing, rhythmic creaking of her apron as she breathed, and the pleasure of being with her, that prevented me from rejecting any further treatment.

"We'll soon be done now, pet. It won't be much longer. You'll have a nice clear head to wash in the bath tonight."

It was Mrs. Samuel's day off. Mrs. Parrot would be bathing us. It ought not to be a day for nits.

84

"We have some forms to be filled in," Miss Bailey was saying. "It's to do with ration books, identity cards and suchlike. When we've finished this job, we'll see to them. You have to write your name."

I think about my name. I have only one first name. Goody is Joyce Joan. Lots of people have two names. I was christened Antoinette. What a useless name. First they'd tried to call me by a boy's name, Toni, and now I'm Cab. I should have been called Rose. I like the name Rose. The princess is called Rose. Miss Bailey breaks into my thoughts.

"There you are. All done. Let's go and do those forms."

It was something to do with people knowing who you were. I had to write my name.

"Can you write your own name here?"

"If you tell me how to spell it, 'cos my name's hard. I only have to write Ann at school."

"Yes, it is rather a big name," she agreed. "Antoinette, isn't it?"

"Antoinette Rose Savage," I said with a burst of impulsiveness. Well, why not? My name was mine.

"Are you sure about that?" She didn't sound convinced.

"Oh yes. It's just that nobody ever uses my proper name," I said bitterly.

My enlarged name was duly recorded on the forms. It put the final polish on a lovely day.

When the summer holidays came, Mrs. Samuel took us swimming. Once a week we set off on the long walk to

Shere. Shere was a small hamlet, but it boasted a swimming pool. It was about a mile further on than school with a choice of route to get there. On the days that we went through Albury Park, we didn't have to wait to get to the pool to get wet. Quite a full stream sparkled down towards Shere and in the last meadow before the village road there was a low waterfall. A curved, stone slab gave the stream a step down to a lower level. Our shoes were ripped from our feet as we ran. We leaped into the bubbling coldness of the waterfall or balanced along the top of the slab. The water gurgled between our hot toes as we wobbled, precariously, on the weed-slippery ledge. It made the remaining walk to the pool bearable.

Part way along the village road was a white wall of a large windowless building. At this point we would all stop breathing for as long as we could hold out. The smell was atrocious. The boys said the smell was like "rotten eggs", and that it was a factory. No-one could explain why it smelled so foul. By the corner, where we turned to enter the pool, was a tea room called the Copper Kettle. A lovely smell of freshly baked bread wafted through the open door. We stared at the people sitting having afternoon tea. What they must have thought at the sight of us can only be imagined. We must have looked a lot cleaner on the return trip.

The swimming pool was completely hidden behind tall, corrugated-iron fencing. There was a low turnstile where you paid to go in. The water was usually green, sometimes very green, because it wasn't cleaned very often. Being so well sheltered by the fence, it was never too cold. Rows of wooden cubicles with tatty curtains lined either side and, at the far end, a full-sized revolving gate supplied the only exit. Such a narrow strip of edging surrounded the water that it was surprising that none of us ever fell into the water fully clothed. None of us could swim, but we enjoyed trying to learn.

Provided we kept to time, we caught a bus back to the top of Newlands Corner. If we promised to walk in complete silence, we were led through the grounds of the big hotel which stood right on the top of the hill. It saved a much longer walk home.

A cool place to visit was the Silent Pool. It was, in fact, quite close to school, but on our side of the Shere road. We would walk the Pilgrims' Way which followed the top ridge of the Downs until we reached the path leading down to the pool. The route went through deep beech woods which were cool and shady. There was one entrance through a wooden, swing gate. Unless you went through this gate there was no other way you would ever find the secret of the hill.

A little leaf-strewn pathway led gently upwards, deeper and deeper into dense woodland. It was dark and very cold. Abruptly, it was as if the trees had stepped back to form a vast cavern containing a lake. The water was as ice, glassily smooth. It was the most incredible blue, not quite aquamarine, not quite sky blue. (*The pool is no longer blue. Fertilizers must have washed down into the water table over the years. Algae and weeds flourish, covering the white chalk of the bottom so that the pool now looks like any ordinary pond.)*

The path went right round the pool, rising at the furthest end where it was high above the water. Here, when you looked down, the pool seemed to be fathomless. The fable was that it was bottomless. A young girl was supposed to have drowned in its awesome chilliness whilst trying to escape in a boat. The descent on the far side proved the story. There, where the path came down to the water's edge, in the chalky, sandy shallows was a sunken boat. Walking around the pool was very scary. No birds sang, no wind blew and it felt as if it was a deeply magical place. Once outside again, in the strikingly warmer air, speculation and exaggeration kept us occupied all the way home. It was the stuff of nightmares.

If getting us all healthily exhausted was Mrs. Samuels' intention, then the trips to Clandon were the most successful. It was a hard walk down into the valley, with no alternative to a long stretch of hot, feet-hurting pavement. The goal was the children's playground. It occupied a field behind a hedge alongside a road, in complete isolation. I could never fathom why it was there in the middle of nowhere. It contained an unusually wide selection of equipment. There were swings, a rocking horse, roundabouts of different designs and slides. One of the slides was tremendously high. It had a roofed box at the top of the stairs, which made it feel a bit safer when up there. The brass slide had a hump halfway down which made it too scary for me to use more than once. We were allowed to stay until we were satiated. Each time we went, the realisation of the long uphill journey home didn't dawn until we'd worn ourselves out.

"Can't we catch a bus?" we all moaned.

"No. There isn't one going our way."

"Couldn't Mr. Raven come and get us in the car?" someone asked hopefully.

"No. Of course not. Come on. It's really not very far. You just think it is."

The school holiday also means that Peggy is available. She often joins us on our walks, but isn't always free to play.

"Hey. Let's go down and see if Peggy can play," suggests Runci. Valerie, Goody and I readily agree. The boys have gone off on some secret activity and we've been told we're not wanted. The normal way to the cottage is along the drive and down the track. We rarely go that way. It's much more interesting the back way. The little left hand pathway at the bottom of the woodland ride, which leads to Peggy's back gate, is a real obstacle course. The cess pit often overflows across this path. The greyish, khaki sludge oozes down the sloping copse to carve channels in our path. Nettles grow in thriving abundance and brambles lie in wait for the unwary. The stench can be overpowering. Long jumping, slipping, ducking and dodging, we challenge Nature's efforts to block our way. Torn, stung and soiled, we triumphantly reach the gate and begin to shout,

"Peggy, Peggy, are you there?"

She is at home, sitting in the garden in the sunshine.

"Will you play with us?" pleads Valerie.

"It's far too hot to play today. I'm broiling hot doing nothing. Come and sit with me," she invites us with a smile of welcome, "You all look like you've been boiled!"

"Would you all like a drink of lemonade?" Mrs. Parrot asks, leaning out of her kitchen window.

"Ooo, yes, please," we reply in unison.

The drink is deliciously refreshing, but makes us aware of just how hot we are.

"I wish we had somewhere to paddle," Goody sighs.

"That would be lovely," Runci agrees, "Mmm, having your feet in cold water would soon cool you off."

"You could always put you feet in our water butt," suggests Peggy. "They can, can't they, Mum? It's what I used to do when I was little."

"I don't see why not. You'll have to take turns, mind, and you'd better take off your clothes."

"Not all our clothes," I protest. "You don't mean all our clothes. Someone might see."

"All right. You can leave your knickers on," Mrs. Parrot chuckles, "But put the rest of your clothes where they won't get wet." This butt is our size. Peggy removes the lid and lifts us in, one at a time. Our heads and shoulders just protrude over the edge so that when we hold on to the rim we can bounce up and down quite safely. It is wonderful. We each emerge a bit green stained but much cooler. I am squealing with delight in the middle of my second go when I catch sight of my

90

Gran. She wears a horrified expression and her voice is colder than the water.

"Is that you, Ann? Get out of there, at once."

"Now here's your Gran, come all this way to visit you," says Mrs. Parrot soothingly as she lifts me out.

"But I want to stay. I don't want to get out."

"Don't be a silly. Your Gran don't often get to see you, so get your things on quick like and go and tell her all your news."

I am reluctant to leave the game, but happy to have my Gran, until she starts complaining.

"I don't know what you were thinking of, really I don't." She scolds as we plod up the track. "Filthy. Absolutely filthy."

"No, it wasn't. It was clean. It was rainwater. Giggy washes in rainwater," I protest hotly.

"Well, you just look at yourself, Miss. The germs that must be in that butt. You could be ill," she tut tuts.

My pleasure slides down the scale into misery as words surround me: unladylike; dangerous; ragamuffin; wild. We arrive at the parlour where everyone tries to restore all the happy feelings a visit should have. With a nice cup of tea and a comfy chair, Gran is recuperating. I feel loving and loved as I chatter away. I hear Miss Bailey say, "We'll have to go through the papers before you go today, Mrs. Savage."

"Oh yes, Miss Bailey. We'd better do that now. Such a nuisance all this *mumble, mumble, mumble* ANN. WHAT IS THIS?" Startled into shock, I say "What?" I have no idea what is coming.

"You know very well what."

There is fury in Gran's voice.

"Your name is not Rose. You know very well you're not Rose. Whatever possessed you to do such a thing?"

On and on she goes. I try to explain. They don't seem able to understand. How can it hurt to leave it. It can't matter. They say something about not getting any rations if you're not registered properly as they busily scratch and scribble. Nothing more is said, or happens. It doesn't need to. I can't feel more miserable.

Although we were not in the least concerned about our appearance or what we wore, there were times when our sensibilities were offended. We all had "pudding basin" haircuts to ease the battle with head lice. Our clothes depended entirely on war-time availability, for clothes were rationed. Clothes were supplied by our families, suitably hard-wearing and functional.

Pudding basin haircuts were the first thing to be viewed with distaste. As the name implies, a china pudding basin was placed on our heads and any hair below the rim was cut off. The result was a uniform, short style, with no concession to personality or fashion. We were told that we would not pick up lice with clean, short hair. In fact that is exactly the sort of hair that lice prefer.

Suddenly we noticed that the boys were going to a proper barber in Albury for their hair cuts. They had really short men's cuts. This was an indignity which grew as we began to notice people's hair. Girls at school had styles. Plaits, bunches, fringes or loosely long, their hair was attractive. Worse, we still got the dreaded infestations. Our arguments fell on deaf ears, so we became resigned to horrible hair.

Our clothes only varied for summer or winter wear. The boys had vests, pants, long or short socks, short grey trousers, either long or short sleeved shirts, ties, jumpers and jackets.

The girls had more differences in their seasonal clothes. In winter we wore vests, liberty bodices, navy bloomers, socks, skirts or thick dresses, shirts, jumpers and coats. The liberty bodices were like waistcoats of loosely knitted cotton. They had a fluffy lining and rubber buttons down the front. When we were old enough to wear stockings, and these were of thick lisle, the bodices came with rubber suspenders attached for fixing to the stocking tops. Bloomers were baggy woolly knickers with elastic at the waist and below the knees. In the summer we gave up wearing both of these articles, and wore ordinary knickers instead which were like cotton shorts. Also, we changed into cotton dresses, or shorts and blouses.

Shoes were not a matter of choice either. My feet grew large very quickly. Several times I had to wear second-hand shoes because none could be found in my size. Nothing was worse than having to wear boy's shoes though. I really suffered until their obvious newness and identity wore off with ill treatment. Then I could forget about them. To be given something new, and preferably pretty, to wear was thrilling for five minutes. Whatever it was, it soon lost its new look.

CHAPTER
TEN

Pouring over the hill in a startle of noise, we stop absolutely dead in our tracks.

"Cor. Just look at that!" says Brian.

The field beside the wire behind the kitchen garden hedge is packed from edge to edge with army vehicles and equipment. Canvas-topped lorries, jeeps, tents, and field guns draped with camouflage netting meet our bewildered gaze.

"Where'd they come from? What're they doin' here? Who said they could be on our field?" With the air resounding with unanswered questions we continue down the hill to seek explanations. The answers we get don't really satisfy our curiosity. The soldiers are allowed on the field. They do have permission, and no-one knows for how long they will be staying.

"You're not to make a nuisance of yourselves," we are told. "The soldiers are very busy. They have work to do. They won't want you pestering them."

We comply, but take to using the drive and the track, instead of the hill path so as to gain a good view of what is going on. A row of lorries is parked with their backs towards the drive. Several soldiers are busy in or around them. They wave to us. We wave back. They shout, "Hello, Charlie", or whatever name comes into their heads, in that particular way that any group of working men will address passers-by. These cheerfully shouted greetings soon encourage us to venture closer. It isn't long before we each make new friends.

My special pal is Dave. I grow very fond of him. I give him a welcoming shout on my way to school, and rush to see if he's not too busy to chat on my way home. At first, I lean on and peer over the tailboard of his lorry. All my questions are answered properly. Dave has children of his own. He shows me their photographs. I tell him about my Dad.

"A Sergeant Major, eh?" he says. "He's an important man, your Dad."

I learn about the Army. The different roles and status of the different ranks give me an understanding of the job my Dad has to do. Dave is a mechanic. He is expected to be able to repair anything. He lifts me up into the back of his lorry to explain all the equipment. There's a workbench fitted with two vices. His tools are hung, or neatly laid out, ready for use. There are sheets of metal, rolls of wire, cans of all kinds and two big oil drums. We sit on the drums to talk.

"I have to fix broken engines, straighten wheels and find a way to repair anything that gets damaged," he tells me. "When you're in battle you can't wait for spare parts. Things have to be fixed quick. Can't hang about. That's my job. I have to keep things moving any way I can. I usually manage to make something up."

I'm fascinated because this is my philosophy. I've met a fellow believer in the possibility of things. Seeing

Dave becomes the most important part of the day. If he's free, I spend time with him. If not, I do something else to fill in the space. I watch him working while we talk. He uses tin snips, cutting deftly along precise markings scored on sheets of metal. He hammers, twists, bends and files metal into parts of all shapes and sizes.

"Can I try to make something?" I urge one day. He considers for a moment, and then decides,

"I don't see why not. What do you want to make? Have you any ideas?"

"Could I make a box. A small box to put things in?"

"That should be easy enough," he agrees. "You come and see me tomorrow and, if I'm not busy, we'll see what we can do."

He is waiting for me when I get back from school the next afternoon. He lifts me up into the workshop and shows me a piece of tin.

"This will do for you. We'll have to cut it out so's it will make a box when it's folded up. Then we'll solder the edges to join the sides together."

I'm convinced that I am making it, and thrilled with the creativity of the task. In truth, Dave drew the net and scored the cutting lines. I am allowed to cut the easy bits, using the vice to hold the metal steady. We hammered the metal gently into shape. I held the solder whilst Dave sealed the seams. At last we had completed a box which had a perfectly fitting lid as well.

"Needs a lick of paint now," he says. "I'll see what I can find. Leave it with me for a few days."

The next time he is free to see me, he has some white paint and a brush ready and waiting. My box has a smooth dull grey finish like the nasturtium tank.

"I undercoated it for you the other day," Dave explains. "The white paint wouldn't have stuck on properly without it."

He shows me how to apply the paint. I brush it on very carefully, both inside and out. When I've finished, he says,

"It will take quite a few days to dry off really hard. I'll take care of it for you. I'm going to be very busy for a while, too, so you come back next week."

The camp seems to change during the following days. Vehicles are moved to different positions, engines are constantly revving up and the soldiers moved about more purposefully with no time for banter. We all feel this atmosphere of seriousness.

"They're getting' ready to move," Peter states flatly. "They tole me they was movin' on soon."

"Where are they goin'?" I don't want to believe him. We have accepted the Army's presence as permanent by now.

"I don't know. They didn't know."

"They're goin' to fight the war, that's for sure," says Brian. "We won't see them again."

At last I see Dave by his lorry.

"Dave, Dave, are you busy?"

"No. Come on, Ann, your box is dry now. You can have it." He hands me the glossy cuboid of white metal of which I am so proud.

"Thank you, Dave. Thank you ever so much. It's lovely. Is it true you're goin' away?"

He tells me quietly, yes, he's going, but he doesn't know exactly when. I don't need to worry about him in the war. He's always at the back, mending things, so he won't be in the front where it's dangerous. He gives me a hug.

"I will miss you, when you're gone," I sigh.

"I'll miss you too, Trouble," he replies.

"Will I ever see you again?"

"I've no idea," he says with honesty. "Perhaps we'll be back this way sometime. You never know. Anyway, see you tomorrow."

"Yes. See you tomorrow, then. Thanks for my box." I kiss his cheek.

Upstairs, I'm like Eeyore with his balloon. I put things in my box and then take them out again. Eventually I put all my small treasures in it and put on the lid.

When we get up the next morning, the field is empty. It's as if no-one has ever been there. Nothing remains to console us — except my little tin box.

A new girl has arrived at school. Her name is Christine and she is ethereal. Blonde, petite and pretty, she quickly gathers an entourage of admirers. I am tall for my age but now I feel abnormally big and awkward, she is so dainty. She evokes protectiveness from those around her. I hover in the wake of her admiring followers for days. I take an unaccustomed interest in my appearance. I wear my most treasured possession, a necklace of tiny cut-glass beads. The beads are coloured speedwell blue. They are threaded together with twists of copper wire. The necklace is very versatile because it is so long. It can be worn as a many-stranded bracelet, necklet or tiara. It sparkles in the light. Christine notices it immediately.

"Ann, what a pretty necklace. Here, come and sit by me. May I look at it?" I take it off and give it to her.

"Can I wear it for a while, Ann?"

"Yes, of course." I swallow the lump in my throat. "You can wear it all day, if you like." I'm a Bottom to her Titania, but it cannot last. She flits from friend to friend as a butterfly samples flowers. I wallow in her golden glow for a few short days, pine when she plays with someone else, and return to join in with the skipping group.

The gardens at school were beautiful. To an awestruck townie, they were magical. Once through the shrubbery of the curving path which led from the church avenue to the rear of Cook's Place, the gardens lay ahead looking like a picture on a chocolate box. A smooth lawn sloped down along the edge of the path. It levelled about a metre below the path and was probably a croquet lawn. Between the house and the lawn were rose beds. A spindle tree, aflame with pink seed pods when we first arrived, grew at the corner. The rest of the garden was laid out with grassy walkways around beds of flowers which blazed with colour. At the furthest point was a spinney of evergreens which included some splendid rhododendrons. We were not allowed to go to the front or the far side of the house. We played on the lawn or amongst the trees. We found quiet corners to sit in and socialise. The day that I suddenly became aware that the lawn had gone remains a picture in my head. Where there had been grass was now a brown, shiny slope, sliding down to a smooth, hard, dark brown plateau. I felt sad and guilty. Miss Hall assured me that the grass would grow again when we no longer played there. I ceased to notice it after that.

Adults often become wildly enthusiastic about a game or a pastime which can hold their interest for life, whilst for children many activities are temporary crazes, particularly the old traditional ones. We all became involved in each craze as it arose. Many were aborted by the girls who were easily daunted by failure. If the boys failed in a skill, such as skipping, they excused themselves by calling the activity sissy.

To perfect a decent bow and arrow required a determined effort. The result became almost predictable. If the bowstring was too taut, the bow snapped or split. If the bowstring wasn't taut, the arrow plopped derisively at your feet. Even when success was achieved, one good shot would either stretch the string or weaken the bow. Obviously Robin Hood knew more about hazel trees than we did.

Peashooters were easily cut from hollow wild parsley stems. The art of blowing a dried pea with enough force to be of use, let alone with accuracy, somehow eluded most girls. Defenceless, they kept their distance from the boys until they had lost interest.

At home we all collected marbles. We kept them in tins ready to use when the time for marble games came round. I did excel in an ability to throw and could hit a target with a stone more successfully than most boys. Hence, for ball games, I was always put in the outfield. I gloried in my ability to throw a retrieved ball a long way with accuracy. Whilst my attempts at whistling drew utter scorn.

We wasted hours trying to produce conch-like notes, blowing through wide blades of grass tightly gripped between thumb edges. There was no pleasure in the odd, pitiful squeak I sometimes made, when Goody could shake the trees with the resonance of her note. Neither could I master either the two- or four-fingered whistles. Those who developed this skill produced unbelievably loud, shrill whistles far superior to those of the metal ones in the shop. In bouts of determination I would sit with Goody under instruction, nearly bursting with the effort to make a whistle. Usually one of the adults would insist that we stop, their nerves racked, their patience exhausted. All I ever had to show for my energies was a stream of dribble coursing down my arms and dripping off my elbows.

"Come here and get ready. Quickly," calls Mrs. Samuel, gathering us with her voice. "We're going for a walk." A groan greets her words. "Where would you like to go today?" she asks.

We confer amongst ourselves, in the unique way that children do. It then turns into a Dutch Auction where we all shout our choices whilst considering others' suggestions at the same time. We finally reach a majority decision where you win some and lose some.

"We want to go to the tree house again. The film star's house," the winners dictate.

"He might be there this time," Runci says hopefully. I remember that I still haven't found out how the owners of the house actually get to it. In answer to my question, Mrs. Samuel guesses, "I think that they must go along the Pilgrims' Way. We'll go by that way today."

Up the hill we troop. Plover's Field is now full of ripening mangelwurzels. It reminds us that we haven't tried eating those yet. We turn left, following the wide, grassy way. The trees, mostly of beech, begin to grow more densely on either side. This is the same woodland which envelops the tree house and which extends down to the Silent Pool. Suddenly the boys, who are up front as usual, begin to shout,

"Hey. Just come an' look at this. There's bombs 'ere. Piles of bombs!"

"An' ammo boxes!" yells Fitz, as we run to see.

"Don't touch anything. Don't go near," orders Mrs. Samuel. "You are to keep on the path. We can walk on the path."

Walking with lighter tread, we rake either side of the way with astounded eyes. There are huge piles of petrol cans. Pile after pile, neatly set out with wide walkways between. Similarly laid out are hundreds of stout boxes quite unmistakably of ammunition. The bombs, with their fat, conic ends towards us, lie in groups. As we walk, there seems no end to the dump. The wood is broodingly silent over this hoard of things which kill.

"We'll all get blown up," I whisper, in terror. "They'll explode if we shake the ground."

"Stop that, Ann. Stop it at once." Mrs. Samuel is cross. "They can't blow up by themselves. They have to be dropped or fired. Nothing here can hurt us. It is only here, hidden, until the soldiers come to take it all away."

The fact that we have now reached clear woodland and are obviously past the end of the dump relieves me much more than her assurances. Once at the tree house, it is all forgotten. The house is still deserted, to our disappointment. We return across the fields.

It was on the way to school that we noticed the arrows. As we crossed over the Pilgrims' Way, we saw a black arrow marked on a square, white board. It was attached to a short post, low in the grass, and the arrow pointed in the direction of the dump. A quick reconnoitre in both directions disclosed arrows placed at regular intervals. They were all pointing the same way. As far as we could tell, they were placed the whole length of the route from the main road to the dump. We quietly speculated about them all the way to school.

"It's spies," I opine. "It's German spies."

"The arrows show the way to the dump," Peter says, "so's the soldiers can see where to go to collect it."

"Why would they need to put arrows? They must know where they put the stuff," argues Goody.

"See. Then it must be spies," I conclude. "That proves it. They're to show Jerry the way so's he can blow it all up."

We continued to debate the problem. We were all aware of the campaign which the government had organised. All public places had notices with slogans warning people not to disclose any secrets. They carried one liners: "Be Like Dad, Keep Mum"; "Careless Talk Costs Lives" and so on. So it was not surprising, whilst pondering about spies, that Mrs. Samuel came under our suspicion. How this happened can only be imagined but by the time we arrived at school, we'd decided that she was a German spy, marking out with arrows all the secret places. We concluded that was the reason we kept going on all those long walks.

I can only conjecture about how the mountain grew out of this molehill. Most probably the story spread amongst the schoolchildren. Some must have related the story to their foster families. It must have been these adults who fertilised the seed of our nonsense, causing it to grow to alarming proportions. The first we knew that something terrible was about to happen was a visit by the police. The adults were gathered together in the parlour. We were all summoned to the playroom shortly afterwards. With the exception of Mrs. Samuel and Ralph, everyone stood waiting for us to line up. We were subjected to quite a diatribe, containing many unforgettable words. Cruel, Wicked, Hurtful, Unthinking and Hateful were some. "You will sit and think about what you have done. You will go to apologise as soon as you have thought, really thought, about the pain and sadness you have caused."

There was much more. I was left in no doubt that to label a person a spy was a very serious thing indeed. We could have got Mrs. Samuel shot. She must be very unhappy. When I went to say how sorry I was, Mrs. Samuel was sitting by the window of her room. She looked terribly sad.

"I'm very, very sorry for sayin' you was a spy," I wailed, and burst into tears.

"It was a terrible thing to say," she said. "You wouldn't quite understand. Although Germany is my home, and I have friends in great danger there, I am on your side. I love England. Ralph and I are here, like you are, to be safe from the war."

We then hugged each other. She gave me a chocolate button from a little glass dish on her dressing table.

"Run along now, and forget about it," she said quietly. We were all pretty docile, for a time.

The arrows disappeared one night, for in the morning they were gone. Out walking, some time later, we discovered that the dump had gone too. No trace of it was left. We couldn't even agree on where we thought it had been.

CHAPTER
ELEVEN

It was just as well that we had discovered the removal of the weapons dump along the Pilgrims' Way because we would have been very frightened indeed when we saw a dump blowing up. Perhaps it was the sound of the explosions, or maybe news of the event had reached us, which caused us to investigate. We all went to watch from the viewpoint at Newlands Corner. From this point one could see miles of countryside spread out like a map. On the southern horizon, where a line of trees met the sky, a pall of ugly black smoke billowed. We could hear bangs, rumbles and cracking noises almost continuously. We could see brilliant bursts of flame which seemed unrelated to the explosions heard. Horrific mushrooms of red and yellow fire leapt skywards, died down, and resurged. The explosions did not coincide with the flames. It was my first remembered science lesson. What a way to learn that light travels faster than sound and that the distance could be estimated. (*Each second of delay between a flash and a bang is approximately one mile of distance.*)

"One, and a two, and a three, and a four," we all droned. The really large explosions gave the best results. Our agreed estimations judged the inferno to be about five or six miles away and the area to be around Abinger Hammer. The boys speculated excitedly about the cause of each eruption.

"Bet that was a bomb blowin' up."

"Nah, it must've bin a heap of petrol cans. Just look at those flames."

Bombs or petrol, it was too awful to contemplate. I presumed that all the little cracking sounds were of bullets bursting from their boxes.

"What about all the people over there?" I asked Mrs. Samuel. "Are they going to be killed?"

"The dump isn't near anybody, Ann. You don't have to worry. Anything dangerous would be hidden right away from where people live, like the dump we found once."

"What made it catch light?" I voiced another fear.

"It probably started by accident. Bright sunlight shining through a piece of broken glass can begin a fire. We'll hear all about it when the news gets to us," she said soothingly. We were led away then, back to our familiar, less imaginative surroundings.

Just inside our woodland, halfway down the drive, were two wooden buildings. One was a tall structure with huge, barn-like doors. It looked as if it was a giant's shed. Facing it, the other building was a summer house with a name board that read CANADA. It must have been unbearable for the adults when we were forced to be in the playroom, so Canada was unlocked for our use. In the holidays, it gave shelter in showery weather and prevented the need for us to be continually trooping in and out with muddy feet.

The front aspect of Canada would not have looked out of place in a wild west film. It had the railed balcony, central doorway and small square windows which are always a feature of westerns. Inside was a simple, square room with a window at either side. There was an old wooden table in the middle. Piled up in the far corner were some garden chairs, grey with age. The fun of playing inside the summer house palled very quickly. It was, however, a useful meeting place, somewhere to plan activities whilst waiting for the weather to clear up. Conversely, it was pleasantly cool on a hot summer day.

Having returned from watching the exploding dump, we sat, legs a-dangle, along the balcony. We were undecided what to do, except for Goody who was happily revolving herself around the balcony rail.

"What are we goin' to do, then?" Peter asks, impatient to be doing something.

"Let's go an' see Peggy," Valerie suggests, as she always does. "She'll think of something for us to do."

"Look at ol' Raven's shed," Brian says speculatively, "He's left the doors open. I wonder what he uses it for."

His comment makes us all aware of the obvious. The barn doors opposite are ajar, when it's usual for them to be locked with a large padlock.

"It's ever so big. You could keep a bus in there," observes Fitz. "Let's go an' have a look."

We slide off the balcony and move, cautiously, over to the barn. We sidle in through the crack in the doors. It takes a while to accustom our eyes to the gloom. The only light is from a small window high up near the roof, hooked open to give ventilation. We venture right inside to find that it is as big as Fitz predicted.

"It's full of vegetables," Ralph is unenthusiastic, "Vegetables and garden stuff."

We circle round, finding potatoes, carrots, apples, turnips and swedes, either piled up or laid out on shelving. A pile of neatly folded sacks lies on a shelf. Garden tools lean against the wall and straw is strewn all over the floor from a heap in the corner.

"What are you lot doin' in my shed?"

We spin round guiltily to confront Mr. Raven.

"We was just lookin'."

"Well, you can just keep away. I'm not havin' you muckin' about in 'ere. This's my store for keepin' the winter food. You can go an' play somewheres else. I don't want to catch any of you in 'ere again."

We move quickly, in a group, heading down in the direction of Peggy's back path.

"Yeah. Peggy'll think of somethin' to do."

"Ol' Raven's real grumpy, in't he? We weren't doin' nothin', weren't hurtin' nothin'."

"Here's Peggy! Hey, Peggy, we was just comin' to find you. Where you off to?" We surround her delightedly.

"I was on my way to find you. I thought we could play a ball game."

"Let's go in the chalk pit," suggests Ralph, "It's good in there for practising throwing and catching."

Opposite Mrs. Parrot's cottage is a break in the downland scrub which gives access to the pit. From the entrance it looks as though a giant has taken an enormous bite out of the hillside. A grassy floor slopes slightly back towards the base of the gleaming white semicircular chalkface. To us, it is an exciting cliff. Lush grass surrounds the sides and edges of the pit. It forms a useful barrier, saving a lot of leg work in whatever ball game we choose to play. It is very hot so after a while we flop down on the grass to rest. The boys never sit for long. Today they decide to try to climb up the chalkface. For every three steps gained they slide back two. With rugged determination Brian and Ralph finally make it to the top where they sit proudly on the edge, yelling encouragement.

"Come on. It's easy once you get goin'. Come on, Peter." When Peter reaches their helping hands and is hauled up to join them, we can't resist this new challenge. Fitz has chosen a particularly slippery route. When he manages to get halfway up, he begins to slip back down. He can't stop and he slides all the way back to the bottom. Complaining bitterly about his hands and knees, he decides instead to crawl up the grassy perimeter to the top. Meanwhile, Goody makes the climb with ease, whilst Runci and Valerie go up via the grass. I'm determined that I will succeed however long it takes. I choose the roughest route I can find, so as to have a better grip on the steep surface of the chalk. It is very difficult. The shouts of encouragement urge me to greater effort.

"Come on, Cab. You can do it. You're nearly here."

"Move over to this side a bit more," I hear Goody's instructions above the hubbub, "It's easier over here."

110

I'm sweaty, tired and not a little frightened when, just out of reach of their willing hands, I begin to feel my foot slipping. Transferring my weight to the other foot, I stretch up for a more secure foothold and lunge with a fatalistic grab for the cluster of hands fishing to catch mine. We make contact. I'm trawled up to the safety of the ledge above.

"Well done, Cab. You made it." I glow with pride at my achievement. I sit in a dreamy state of euphoria until I begin to be aware of the proposals now under discussion.

"Should be easy if we squat on our heels an' take it slow. The middle bit's best. That's really smooth."

"It can't hurt through our shoes. We'll be slidin' on our feet."

"You're not goin' to slide down?" I ask, already realising the answer. It will need more daring than I think I can muster.

"Course we are. It'll be easy, you watch."

Brian lowers himself over the edge slowly. Squatting, he jerkily slips down the chalkface on his feet, with his bottom breaking his progress intermittently. On arrival at the base, he leaps up exultantly to yell how great it is, how easy it is. I move back a metre. Ralph goes next, followed by Goody who immediately crawls back up the grassy side shouting her intention to have another go. This obvious enthusiasm spurs Fitz to try. When he manages to accomplish the slide in safety, his success gives us greater reassurance than the mere words of the acknowledged daredevils among us.

"S'easier goin' down," he calls. "Honest. It's good, really good."

We all try. He's right. The slide becomes smoother and shinier with each descent. There is no requirement now to climb the face. Ascending by way of the grassy side is acceptable, once you've proved yourself. So we crawl up and slide down, a little faster each time. We do follow each other at sensible intervals, but could not have foreseen the accident. We only spot a flint, dislodged from the edge, when it's half way down. Valerie is just approaching the bottom. We scream for her to look out. The diminutive figure in her white, peasant blouse and shorts seems to be frozen, as in a photograph. The flint hits the small of her back. Her cry of pain shatters the moment, and we rush to help. Peggy reaches her first, gathering a sobbing Valerie in her arms. A bump has already swollen above her bottom. The shock of the unexpected blow has frightened her a lot.

"I'll take her to my Mum. She'll make it feel better. I don't think you should slide any more. It could be dangerous if a flint were to hit you on the head."

We all agree with Peggy. We are quite sobered by the event. We straggle towards the road as Mr. and Mrs. Stringer appear on our horizon. Their expressions are familiar to me. They are looking at us in the same way that my Gran looked at me when I was in the water butt. Brian and Peter walk up the road with them, whilst the rest of us troop across to Peggy's. Mrs. Parrot examines Valerie's back.

112

"Oh, t'isn't so bad," she soothes. "A little butter will soon make it better."

"Butter," we echo incredulously.

"Yes, butter. It helps to oil the swelling."

Mrs. Parrot persuades Valerie to bend over an armchair, dabs a bit of butter on the bump and then presses it with the cold, wide, flat blade of a knife. She explains that this will help to make the swelling go down. Given a drink of water and a wipe over with a flannel, Valerie is quite recovered. Now we come under scrutiny.

"Just look at you. You can't go back up the hill like that. We'd better get you cleaned up a bit."

We contemplate each other. We are whitely chalk dusted over grime. This sudden awareness of our terrible appearance comes as a complete surprise. One by one we are wiped over at the sink, having first been ordered outside to pat the dust from our clothes. Eventually, much tidier, we are dispatched to go the road way home. The realisation of my good luck dawns as we walk. What if Gran had come today. I wonder what Mr. and Mrs. Stringer said to Brian and Peter. We scamper along the drive to take up our positions on the kitchen steps.

The last few precious days of the summer holidays turn our thoughts once more to food. We've tried groundnuts and found them tasty. The harvest of sweet chestnuts and hazelnuts are not quite ripe. On return to school it will be the conker season. Our supplies are plentiful, but inedible. Goody, Runci, Valerie and I sit patiently, idly, making fishbones from horse chestnut leaves. Creating the perfect skeleton from the veins of the leaf without breaking it is very difficult.

"Let's go an' see if there's any more ripe blackberries," suggests Goody. Our search takes us past Canada. The boys are there, grouped along the balcony.

"What you doin'?" We climb up to join them.

"We've had an idea, but the door is locked."

"What idea?"

"Well, we thought if the barn had bin open, we could've got some potatoes an apples an' cooked 'em properly in a fire. We didn't do it right last time, but we know how to do it now." Brian sounds convincing. "Anyway, it's no good. The door's shut."

"We'll have to watch and wait now till the door's left open," adds Ralph.

"They might never be left open again," Goody says logically. "Not after Mr. Raven found us all in there. There must be another way to get in."

I consider the problem. Beside the barn the peat is kept, stacked, ready for winter. Although depleted, awaiting fresh supplies, there is still a fairly large heap of the weathered and greening blocks. Above is the window.

"We can build steps of peat," I announce positively. "A staircase up to the little window. It's open. Someone could climb up an' get in easy."

"It is only a little window," Brian observes thoughtfully, "They'd have to be small."

"And good at climbing," adds Fitz.

We all look at Goody. "I'll only do it if you promise to keep a proper watch out for ol' Raven. I'm not goin' to get caught pinchin' his stuff, so you've got to let me know if he's comin'."

We all vow to protect her. We arrange to have a line of lookouts as an early warning system. Mollified, she agrees to try the plan. We all help to pile up the peat blocks into a rather rickety staircase. All eyes are on Goody as she tries it out. The structure wobbles alarmingly as she makes her way up the side of the barn.

"It's not very safe. Some of you'd better hold it against the wall so's it don't fall down," she orders.

"Go on. Go on," the boys urge. "Hurry up. We gotta be quick."

Goody has her head and shoulders through the window. Her legs and bottom are all that can be seen. She can be heard mumbling something indistinctly. Something about how is she supposed to get out again, when there is a panic-stricken cry of "Raven is coming".

As we all flee down into the wood, the peat staircase collapses with hardly a sound. I glimpse her entrapment. I hear her complaining. When safely far away, pausing for breath, I don't even feel sorry. Just relief.

CHAPTER
TWELVE

Fitz was always finding things. Whether objects or creatures, he seemed to possess a sixth sense to see things which we didn't notice. He spotted the grass snake from a distance.

"Stop, stop," he commands, "or you'll frighten it away."

"Frighten what?"

"Look. Down there. On the path. It's a whopper."

We inch forward. The snake is large and, at the instant it becomes aware of our presence, very fast moving. It disappears greenly into the long grass of the hillside so quickly that the boys can not rediscover it.

"You can die if they bite you." I am scared.

"Don't be stupid. It was a grass snake. They don't hurt anyone. Adders is the only poisonous snakes and they got black zig zag marks on their backs."

"That one had marks on its back. You could've got killed."

"I'll find you an adder, an' you can see the difference," Fitz promises.

"I don't want to see any snakes. I think they're horrible."

"I think Cab should see an adder," Brian says darkly. "Do her good. She's always scared of something."

I've learnt enough to keep quiet. If I shut up they'll forget about it.

"Hey! Look what I found now," shouts Fitz, waving his hand. The boys huddle around him to get a closer look.

"It's a magnifier," Ralph says with authority.

In the knowledge that it isn't alive, we creep close enough to see. The object is shaped like a tiny lollipop. The lollipop end is of clear glass set into a small, metal, ring. The ring is at the end of a hollow handle which is made so that it can swivel round to encase the glass to protect it. The whole thing is small enough to be held in Ralph's fist.

"Look," he says, opening it out, "If you look at my nail through the glass, it looks bigger. It must be for studying stamps or small things like that."

We take it in turns to experiment with the magnifying theory. Then Brian argues, "It's for lightin' fires. 'Course it magnifies. You hold it in the sunlight and you can get it to burn things."

"Why would you want a thing like that when you got matches?" Goody asks.

"You might run out of matches and it would do till you got some more."

"What good is that if the sun's not shinin'? What about when it's dark?"

"I tell you it's to burn with. Look. If I hold it like this, so's the sun shines through it onto my arm: Cor!

Strewth, that was hot." We all demand to have a go ourselves. There is no doubt it burns.

"Well, let's see if it'll burn dry grass," Fitz suggests. So we all squat in a circle to watch. Very slowly, the patch of dry grass we have chosen begins to smoke. We watch in wonder as it starts to smoulder before finally bursting into flame.

"There, you see," Brian boasts proudly, as he stamps out the blaze, "What did I tell you."

"I think it's a cigarette lighter," Peter says thoughtfully. "'Cos it's war time, they're tryin' to save matches. People who smoke can light their fags with that, an' save matches when it's sunny." It seems a reasonable idea.

"Maybe it was one of those, dropped by somebody, wot caught the bombs alight at Abinger," I suggest.

"Well, we'll have to find out if it will light a fag sometime," Fitz says as he pockets his find.

On the way home from school it is stiflingly hot. Climbing up the last, long, slope, Goody and I dawdle. The warmth rises from the browning grasses, making a heat haze which distorts the vision. Below us, curving in its own route upwards, the metalled road shimmers and appears to be moving. Even the butterflies are still, lazily stretching their wings on the faded wild flowers and undisturbed at our passing. We realise we have got left behind. "Come on. Race you up the last bit," Goody challenges. The boys are at the top, Brian and Peter above the path on one side, with Ralph and Fitz below on the other. I am not suspicious until it's too late. As I level with them they swoop to grab me.

"Leggo. What d'you think yor doin?"

"You're goin' to see wot adders look like. Come on. Pull her over here quick."

I struggle in panic but the impetus of their surprise attack gives me no chance. Before I can even think, I'm pushed head first into a scrubby bush. There are snakes curled in the dappled shade. I cannot absorb any more than that. Before the full horror has time to register, I am yanked backwards and released.

"Now you've seen 'em," they shout laughingly, "P'raps you can tell the diff'rence now." They race away leaving me alone. Goody has wisely made herself scarce. I walk home warily. (They weren't to know that they had planted the seeds of a snake phobia which grew to senseless proportions in adulthood before I could control it.) As it is, my fury at my treatment, with a sense of helplessness of how to prevent the boys from picking on me, leads me to seek out Miss Bailey to complain about them.

"Don't you worry any more about it, Ann. I should think they were just more grass snakes keeping themselves cool. Adders are very shy. It isn't likely that you'd ever see one," she advises. "They were close to the place where you saw the first one this morning, weren't they?"

I agree that is true.

"Well, there you are. They're quite harmless, and now those naughty boys have shown you, they won't bother you again. Try not to let them know about things you don't like. They won't have anything to tease you about then."

I appreciate the logic of her advice, but wonder how I can hide my fear of all the creepy crawlies which seem to be unavoidable. I shall just have to pretend that they don't frighten me. "Can I help you in the kitchen?" I ask hopefully.

"No. There's nothing you can do, pet. I've got a lot to do for a dinner party tonight, so run along now, there's a good girl."

I wander disconsolately across the drive to find someone to play with. Turning the corner by the cellar steps, I hear voices. The boys are huddled together at the bottom of the steps tearing strips of paper.

"What are you doin'?"

"Ssh. Quiet. Come down an' see, only keep quiet."

As I descend I can see they have newspaper and straw. They are trying to roll pieces of straw in squares of paper.

"What's those for?" I whisper.

"We're making fags. If we're goin' to find out if the magnifier will light a fag, we've got to have a fag to light."

"But they're not made of straw, they're made with tobacco."

"We know that, stupid. So where we goin' to get tobacco then? We're just goin' to have to use straw."

"Can I make one?"

"Yeah, course you can. Here." Brian hands me some straw and paper. After trial and error, we discover that the straw has to be split, the paper pre-curled and the bits of straw very carefully laid in the same direction for any hope of rolling a manageable cigarette. Our

120

cigar-like results need many attempts before we think them suitable.

"Let's try them out inside the cellar," suggests Ralph. "No-one comes down here, so we'll be safe."

We gather round the coke stove in the centre. Brian opens the small, hinged door which covers the hole where the coke is shovelled in. There is only a small fire inside because the stove is only needed for domestic hot water at the moment. Using a paper spill, Brian kindles the end of his creation. He puffs cautiously to keep it smouldering. He doesn't complain at the experience, so we all light ours in turn. They burn the tongue and rasp the throat. The smoke stings the eyes. It is all pain.

"Yeuk. They're nasty," say Peter, Fitz and I in unison.

"'Tisn't so bad once you get used to it," Brian says bravely, with his screwed up eyes watering, "'Course, it'd be better if we could get some real cigs. We'll have to get some real ones to try."

We persevere a little longer. It isn't too bad, but it is very hard on the throat. Conspiratorially we burn our traces before creeping back into the sunlight.

A few days later I get a whispered message to meet back in the cellar. Brian proudly produces a small packet of five cigarettes. We each take one and light up. Like young connoisseurs we draw tentative puffs, savour the smoke and discuss our reactions.

"They're not bad. It's a nice taste." We all avidly agree that they are far superior to straw.

"Trouble is they cost a lot of money, and it's not easy to get 'em," Brian muses.

"How did you get 'em?"

"John got a packet in the shop. He lives in the village and gets cigs for his Grandad on his way home. But he can't keep getting' em for us and anyway where we goin' to get the money?"

"I found one today," says Fitz, drawing a battered-looking cigarette from his trouser pocket.

"Cor. Where'd you find that?"

"It was just lyin' on the road, on the way to school. Someone must've dropped it by mistake, but there it was, just lyin' there. I expect people, p'raps the soldiers, drop 'em as they're drivin' along the road. We could keep a look out for more."

"We'll need to have something to keep them in," I suggest, eying his bent prize with scorn. "If we carried a tin box we could keep the ones we find nice and straight."

It is agreed. We each take an old tobacco tin from the playroom cupboard, having found alternative receptacles for marbles, Meccano bits and beads haphazardly. Surreptitiously searching the road twice a day, we find the pickings are rich for we aren't fussy. Half-smoked cigarettes are easy to find. We decide that it's more hygienic just to collect the tobacco. We don't want to catch other people's germs. Each day we meet, in the cellar with our booty. We roll ourselves cigarettes using either newspaper or Bronco lavatory paper to put the tobacco in.

We stopped smoking as suddenly as we had started. Maybe the onset of Autumn made supplies scarce or too wet. Maybe the more frequent use of the cellar prevented opportunity. Whatever it was that altered the routine, we stopped smoking without ever testing the magnifier's power to ignite a cigarette. That was completely forgotten about.

My last confrontation with the boys was over a plum. Looking back, it seemed to mark a point at which we began to be juniors, a point at which the first thoughts about our futures began to form.

We were all given a plump Victoria plum as a treat to take to school for break time. Bursting forth on the unsuspecting countryside, in our usual manner, we made our erratic way up and over the hill. By the time we'd reached the slope down to the Pilgrims' Way, the boys had eaten their plums. I carried mine lovingly in its brown paper bag, savouring the expectancy of eating it later. The boys were making mischievous sallies at the rest of us to force us into eating ours as well. I was the only one who resisted. This prompted their mass attack. One playful grab at my bag didn't miss. I held on, successfully keeping possession, but the plum was squashed and spread on the paper like jam. If, at that moment, I had been consoled or assured that I would get some compensation, I would have thought it "fair". As it was, my anguished cries were met with exhortations to stop that awful noise and to hurry up or we'd be late for school. To add insult to the injury, I was told I should have eaten the plum and then it wouldn't have happened. The sheer power of the sense of injustice was shattering. In an instant it became the vehicle for every remembered grievance and the total was too much to contain. I ran away.

In the bordering hedgerow, a tunnel-like opening offered an impetuous escape route. I went through the bushes into a well-camouflaged ditch. Lying very still, I waited until the sounds of calling for me receded and I was alone in the silence. What to do now? I decided that I could live on sloes, nuts and berries plus any harvest available. It then occurred to me that natural food supplies would fail in the winter. Well, even if I starved then there would be a justice when "they" found my dead body and were stricken with sorrow. All my emotions were sliding into one of deep self-pity. I sat up in my little hiding place, beginning to ache for love, for sympathy, for companionship. Just as I began to stand up, an arm shot through the hedge and a hand grabbed hold of my arm very tightly. I was hauled roughly from my sanctuary, up onto the bank, to face a livid Mrs. Samuel. She was a mass of cold fury which nothing could penetrate. I tried to explain as I was dragged down the hill to school. My words bounced off her, as unheard as her words remained unheard by me.

It was break time when I was summoned to Miss Jones. She had, until now, been someone who was kind and gentle, although regarded with the awe that the young primary child has for their headteacher. When I entered her room she didn't look friendly. By now the morning event had faded into insignificance, leaving a vague doubt as to what might be said at the end of the day. I was not expecting the bombardment of words about my behaviour which Miss Jones unleashed. I could not understand her constant repetition of how

124

serious the matter was nor why on earth my aunt had been summoned because of it.

"I must punish you," Miss Jones was saying. "It hurts me to do this, but you have to be made to understand that it was a very, very naughty thing to do to run away like that. You must never do it again, however wrongly you feel you were treated. Now, hold out your hand."

I saw the cane. I realised the intention. I would not accept punishment when I had lost my plum. It wasn't fair. I snatched the cane from her hand and broke it across my knee in one quick movement. I shouted my rejection of her proposed miscarriage of justice. Miss Jones just looked at me with an expression of amazement. I was made to sit in a corner on a chair, and wait. My chagrin did not subside. After an eternity of waiting, I was taken to see Auntie Bee who had arrived from Windsor. In her loving arms I sobbed myself clean of all the cluttered, mind-fogging, jumble of thoughts and feelings. When tranquillity came, we went outside together to sit on the gazebo. We talked until I could understand the fear and worry I had created by an action which could never have righted the wrong done to me. We sat in the warm sunshine a long time. Once I accepted my own wrongdoing, I had some important apologies to make, which I wanted to make. The feeling about that was good. Sensing the time was right, children began to come close to share my visitor. They enjoyed chatting to my aunt and gave me their unspoken sympathy and friendship. I forgot about the plum. I also grew up a little and became more self-confident.

CHAPTER
THIRTEEN

My married aunt only visited me once. I had not expected her to visit, and I learnt later that she came because Gran couldn't come. We had been bombed. I had been a bridesmaid at her wedding to my Uncle Jack. They came together on one of the last warm days of September.

"We've come to take you out for a picnic. Would you like that?"

"Oh, yes please, Aunty Rene."

"First I want you to try on this new dress we've brought for you, to see if it fits. You've certainly grown since we last saw you." The dress was made of a crisp floral print cotton, mostly blue and white. It had short, puffed sleeves and ties at the waist to make a bow at the back. The fit was perfect. I could hardly take my eyes from my reflection in the mirror.

"Yes. I'm pleased with that." Aunty Rene looked at me approvingly. "Now you shall keep that on and wear your sandals. Wait. Let me put a scarf over your hair. It will stop it blowing about." She tied a silky headscarf on for me. The difference was amazing. "Right, off we go then. Doesn't she look nice, Jack?"

"More like I remember her anyway. Let's go up the hill. I want to take some photographs."

"Is that your camera?"

"Yes. It takes quite good pictures too. If you have photographs they help to remind you of people and places."

Walking with them was different. I was not being taken for a walk, I was going on a picnic. I was on my own ground, able to point out everything that I thought would be of interest. My Aunty Rene loved the countryside. She searched for wild flowers and mini-creatures, expressing delight at each find. We shared our complementary knowledge. We chose a secluded, grassy bank on which to begin our picnic. She had prepared dainty little sandwiches and home-made cakes. There were individual jellies, fruit and some cordial. We sat talking in the warmth of the afternoon whilst Uncle Jack took pictures of the scenery, and of us. I felt like a proper little girl, an individual, for the first time. It was a happy, glowing feeling being just me for a whole day.

Sometime later I was told that they had a baby. They couldn't come again. My new cousin was two before I saw him.

I hadn't had a letter from Dad for a long time. I wrote to him regularly on airmail letters, which were of thin, blue paper that folded up to be an envelope as well. I was getting very worried about him and must have said so in my letters. (After the war we learnt that he had been hit by shrapnel in the back of his neck, and was in a field hospital in the desert.) As soon as he was able to, he sent me a telegram to say he was fit and well. To me, receiving a telegram was the absolute proof that he was safe. I thought that no-one could send a telegram if they were fighting in the war. Everyone paid lip service to my theory. Mrs. Strachey suggested that she should send it to Gran straight away as she had been worried too. Shortly afterwards we were all told that we would be going home for the Christmas holidays because everyone needed a holiday. We all thought that the war must be nearly over.

Goody went to Mr. and Mrs. Turney, the others must have gone to their homes, but my family never knew what to do with me. Grandad was an Air Raid Warden as well as a rent collector, so he wasn't at home to be able to look after me. For Christmas Day and Boxing Day it was thought we'd be safe in London, so Gran, Aunty Bee and I spent it with Grandad. It was a disappointing time. It didn't seem at all Christmassy. We didn't have a tree or decorations. Only the carols broadcast on the radio made it special, but I did find out about all that had happened whilst I'd been away.

A landmine had hit the District Railway line behind our old flat. It had destroyed the back of the house. Grandad was very pleased with himself. He'd always said that the safest place to be in an air raid was behind the open front room door. He said the door would stop the ceiling falling on him. Still, Gran never believed him and worried all the time because he would not go down to the shelters. When the house was destroyed, Grandad was found sitting on a chair behind the door which was the only undamaged part of the house. It was after that experience he became an Air Raid Warden.

Gran had managed to find another flat just around the corner from our old one. To me it seemed exactly the same. We had the upstairs part of another terraced house. We shared the front door with the people downstairs, and the flats were not separated in any way. They just lived downstairs whilst we lived up. They had possession of the back garden. The front wasn't a garden. It was a space with a fat privet hedge behind a front wall. The wall once supported railings and there had been an iron gate, but all the railings and gates in London had been removed to go to make armaments. At least that was what everyone was told at the time. Inside the flat looked the same too. The tiny box room over the hallway was my room. The front room settee was a put-u-up to sleep anyone who needed it. The back bedroom was for Gran and Grandad and the kitchen, once a bedroom, was over the extended back of the house with a tiny bathroom sandwiched in a corner. There was no hot water on tap. The deep stone sink with a wooden draining board was built in the corner of the kitchen next to the bathroom. It had one mains tap. A gas stove was fitted in the opposite corner. A large table and cupboard didn't leave much room to move about. Under the back window was a large oak blanket box with a cushion on it. This had stood in the same place in our old flat, but instead of being able to kneel on it and watch the trains, one could watch people playing tennis on the courts laid in the centre of the land surrounded by the block of terraced houses.

Gran told me that when they opened the chest, after the bomb blast, it was full of broken glass. The wood was undamaged. How the glass got inside the chest without cutting the wood was a mystery which no-one could fathom. The knife grinder and polisher had survived too. This fascinated me because it was impossible to see how it worked. It looked like a solid wooden wheel on legs. In the middle of one side was a handle which could be turned without obviously doing anything. There were three or four fur-lined slits in a row along the top of the wheel. You put a knife into the slit, turned the handle, and the knife got either polished or sharpened.

I also learn that Dad has been with the Eighth Army in the battles of the desert, but that he's now safe in Egypt. The war isn't over and she thinks it will be a long time yet.

I have to go into a hostel until I can return to Guildford. I am beginning to understand the difficulties created by the war. When I am taken back to Harrow Hill Copse, there is a letter waiting for me. Dad's letters to me are usually on the same "fold and stick" air-mail sheets. He can never say very much because he's not allowed to. I am just happy to read that he is well, that he thinks of me and that he hopes it won't be long before he comes home. This letter is a proper one. Inside the envelope with a short note is a photograph of himself. I can't take my eyes away from it. He looks so well, so wonderful. I show it to everyone.

"You'll have to have your photo took to send to him," Mrs. Parrot comments as she admires my picture, "He'd like to see how much you've grown. I don't expect he's got a recent one of you."

"My Uncle Jack's got a camera. He could take one, couldn't he, Mrs. Parrot?"

"Yes, he could take one, but I think you need a proper one done. Like his."

"How do you get one?"

"Well, you goes to a photographer's studio. That's a room where they have special cameras to take really good pictures. We'll have to think about it."

The problem was resolved when my Aunty Bee decided that she would make up for my brief Christmas by spending a weekend with me. She arranged for us to stay in an hotel in Guildford. It was very exciting. The only hotel we knew was the big Newlands Corner one which we sometimes crept past on our way home from the bus stop. It looked very posh. I burned with curiosity to see inside. None of us could imagine what it would be like to stay in an hotel. We expected it to be like a palace. I needed my best clothes for the visit, which would also be suitable to have my photograph taken in.

Granny made most of my clothes. She made sure that I always had a "best" dress which was always outgrown before it was outworn. It was usually made of velvet with long sleeves and a lace collar. That year it was deep blue and already my forearms showed too much below the cuffs. The weather was particularly cold. My dress didn't sit very well over the mass of underclothing: vest, liberty bodice now with bulky rubber suspenders, thick lisle stockings and baggy navy woollen bloomers. I was not very happy having to put socks over my stockings and to wear stout lace-up shoes, but it was better than getting chilblains.

My aunt arrived and took me to Guildford on the bus. It was already growing dark when we arrived, but we managed to walk down to an hotel by the river before it got too dark to see our way. It was the first time that I had been out at night in the wartime blackout. No light showed anywhere. When we entered the hotel lobby, it too was dark. We had to close the outer door before we could go into the main hall. The warmth and light inside was welcoming. We were taken to find our room. All along the passageway, outside the bedroom doors, I noticed that there were shoes. I thought we had to take off our shoes before going into the room. On being told that they were put there to be cleaned I was quite shocked. The thought that someone was going to have to clean all those shoes didn't seem very nice to me. I made a fuss about not wanting to put mine out to add to their work. I felt that it wasn't right.

Mealtimes weren't happy either. The hotel was dark and dingy, not at all like we'd imagined. I had to endure lectures on table manners. Soup spoons should be filled by pushing them away from you, pudding spoons always towards you. I wasn't ready to care about such niceties. Bee probably regretted ever having thought of introducing me to a civilized way of life.

We explored the town and strolled beside the river. We found a photographer half way up the High Street. His studio was along a narrow passageway and up a flight of bare, dusty, stairs. It was a large, empty room.

The man pulled open two long, wooden shutters. Light flooded in, making the room look even bigger and emptier. Worn lino covered the floor. In the far corner was a box on legs. I was told to stand by the window, to keep still. He pulled the box into the middle of the room and then I could see it was a big camera. I supposed you needed a big camera to take big pictures. It didn't take long.

I wish I had been there to see my Dad's reaction to my "studio portrait". I thought it was terrible, especially after the one Uncle Jack took. I looked like an abandoned orphan.

CHAPTER
FOURTEEN

Giggy was in London, Mrs. Samuel was enjoying her day off, and I was enjoying the privacy of convalescence whilst the others were at school.

"You can come and help me, if you like," Mrs. Parrot suggests. "I'm cleaning upstairs today. You can dust."

"Oh yes, please." It seems like the best treat in the world. She gives me a big, fluffy, yellow duster as she tells me what to do.

"Now do it carefully, and slowly. It's no good if I've got to come round behind you and do it all again."

I dust diligently all round our bedroom whilst she mops or vacuums.

"Where does Mrs. Samuel go on her day off?"

"Mostly to her friend's house in Merrow, I think. She needs a break from looking after all of you."

"What do you do when you're not here?"

"I've got my own house to keep clean and tidy, haven't I? Mind you, before the war, we used to get away on holidays. We took Peggy to the seaside when she was small. I don't suppose you remember the seaside. 'Oh, I do like to be beside the seaside. Oh, I do like to be beside the sea'. " She has such a merry voice.

She sings the song through as we work our way out into the passage.

"What is in these rooms of Giggy's, Mrs. Parrot?"

"Oh, yes. I did promise I'd show you, didn't I? They're called dressing rooms, Ann. Ladies have special rooms where they keep their clothes."

I am fascinated. "Why do they need special rooms?"

"Well, you see, they have to own lots of different clothes. All the meetings and things they go to means they can't be wearing the same old things like you and me. I lay out ready whatever Giggy needs to wear, each day. Come. I'll show you." She opens the first door. Steps lead down into a little room. On rails hang rows of clothes. Underneath, neatly paired, are rows of shoes. An ironing board, set up ready for use, stands diagonally across the carpeted floor. There are long mirrors on the wall.

"What's the ironing board there for?"

"She can't put on creased clothes, now can she, silly? If something needs a little press I do it as I lay out for her. That's the job of a Ladies' Maid. I like to do it. Giggy is a very busy, important person. She writes books and today she's in Court. She hasn't got time to be fiddling about with ordinary things."

"And the room next door? What's that for?"

"Ah, well. Gentlemen have dressing rooms too, you see. That was Mr. Strachey's dressing room, but he's dead now, so it isn't needed anymore. I'll show you Giggy's room if you like. She won't mind."

All I can manage to say is "Oh". I can hardly believe that I'm going to be allowed to see inside such a private

135

place. My first impression is of light. There is an outdoor brightness in the room. Three large windows are set into the curve of the enormous bay above the verandah. I feel intrusive just looking at Giggy's bed, Giggy's dressing table. I can see Mrs. Parrot's amusement at my awe. She opens a door in the corner to show me a beautiful bathroom. I'm speechless. Even with cupboards, table and chairs the bedroom is spacious. There are pictures hanging on all the walls. It's a room one could live in. The pictures, in a group beside the door, are the ones I really see.

"Oooh, it's so lovely," I find my voice, "And look at these pictures. They're photographs, aren't they? Oh look. It's the horseshoe. There's children playing. Oh, it's rude! They've got nothin' on." I am very shocked.

"You are a funny one." Mrs. Parrot laughs merrily. "Of course they've got no clothes on. It's hot. It's summer. There's no-one around for miles. Very healthy, that is, letting the sun get on your skin. What is wrong in that?"

I have to admit to myself that it looks natural, happy and fun but I'm not convinced it is proper. "It seems funny to have pictures like that."

"Doesn't your family like pictures of you? You had one took for your Dad. When you're grown up it will be a memory of now. Pictures remind you of what people looked like, of what they did."

"There's a lot of different people."

"Yes. It's a big family. Haven't you looked at all the pictures and paintings around the house? There's two in your playroom. They are portraits of children who

136

lived long, long ago, who belonged to Giggy's family." We go out into the passage, and she closes the door. "You can dust the banisters for me, if you like. I can manage the rest. The banisters need a good hard rub, mind, to bring up the shine."

Down the steps, across the central landing, the door to Mrs. Samuel's room is wide open. Directly in front of me, I can see the dressing table under her window. On top is a glass dish full of chocolate buttons. I have four of them in my mouth before I've even considered the action. I chew once, then swallow in haste for both the fear of being caught and for the shame of breaking her trust. I don't enjoy or really even taste them. I learn in that short moment that there isn't pleasure in thieving. Because I would never dare to admit I have stolen them, I would not be forgiven. Rationing means that everyone can have a little which makes my action worse. I set to the polishing violently, meticulously. I then go to take a long look at those pictures I have not looked at properly before.

When Giggy had visitors, we were instructed not to play around the verandah side of the house so that they could enjoy their privacy. Our routine did not upset theirs, our walks kept us out of the way. When the visitors were her family, they would often introduce themselves to us and spend time with us. I can't remember how they were all related one to another, for some members of the family came rarely. Mrs. Williams-Ellis overwhelmed me by having two surnames. She was business-like, with a resemblance in her manner to Miss Jones. She would always have a

137

conversation with us individually, making us feel of value. Young Mrs. Strachey was pretty, with that attractiveness a truly smiley face bestows and which encourages an approach. She was married to John Strachey. Their two children, Elizabeth and Charles, paid rare visits when, being only slightly older than us, they sometimes joined us to play and teach us new games. They were great fun, completely unselfconscious, gentle and kind. They were also very different from us. Their speech wasn't like ours, their knowledge was wider and, as they both went to private schools, their experiences were vastly different to ours. They were posh. The seeds of the knowledge of a "them" and "us" were sown without rancour.

Our favourite was Mr. John Strachey. He came to see his mother more often. He would always come to have a game with us when staying at the house. In a way, he was the missing link in an otherwise feminine world. He reminded us of what family life should be. He romped with us, swinging us around in circles. He swung us high, delighting us with his strength. We played Tag and He with the tension and excitement of the game making our hair roots ache.

At those times when we kept clear of the verandah area, we would congregate by the seat next to the water butt. It backed onto the house and faced the semicircle of lawn which was the lower part of the "B" to the right of the woodland steps. It wasn't much use to play on. The edge of the lawn was steeply sloped. If a ball went over the edge, someone would have the nasty job of retrieving it. Down in the wilderness below, the rose-bay willowherb was harmless but the stinging nettles, foxgloves and brambles all had their dangers. There was also a well in the furthest corner. Sited on the dividing line between cultivated garden and woodland, it had a wide brick surround. The shaft was protected by a latticed wooden lid set just below the edge inside the well. We would kneel to peer though this, trying to guess the depth by dropping pebbles down into the water. We were often reminded not to go near it. We disobeyed once.

Banned from the horseshoe, we loitered by the butt seat trying to think of something to do. Brian suddenly said he bet he could jump over the well. The warnings that we'd received had made me very nervous about the well. I said he shouldn't do it, rambling on with dire warnings until they forced me to shut up. Sitting on the edge of the seat, petrified he'd fall in, I watched Brian leap over it with ease. Ralph jumped next, clearing it easily and scornfully, before wandering off. Fitz couldn't bring himself to try. He hovered miserably at the side, so Brian shouted, "Come on, Goody, you show him." After a brief assessment of the distance, she too jumped it successfully. Fitz burst into tears of frustration. Peter then took a run up to the well, kicked off from the brickwork and landed with one foot on the far side but the other on the lid. The lid tipped down, swivelling on some central point, making Peter lose his balance. He seemed to topple sideways before slipping down into the gap. He grabbed the edge. I leapt forward screaming and Mrs. Samuel came hurtling round the corner closely followed by Ralph.

After that chastening experience, coupled with a massive telling-off, we stayed clear of the well. Nevertheless, Ralph still had to suffer our taunts of tell-tale. Usually, after things had gone wrong or we'd exhausted a game, we would meander about in ones or twos until a new activity was thought up. At these times we often went to the parlour to ask if there was anything we could do to help. Still upset about the well, I went to the parlour and found Mrs. Parrot busily folding up linen.

"Hello, Ann. There's a little job you could do for me if you like. Would you take these towels up to the back bathroom and put them on the chair just behind the door?"

"You mean the bathroom next to Miss Bailey's room?"

"Yes, that's right. Just put them on the chair."

Happy to be occupied, I trotted off through the hall and up the stairs, barely able to see over the top of the armful of fluffy white towels. Clutching them closely with one arm, unable to see at all now, I groped for the door handle, turned it, pushed open the door and regained both my double hold of the towels and my vision. Transfixed with horror, I found myself facing John Strachey in the bath. He gave a welcoming smile before saying, "Oh good. You've brought my towels up. Thank you very much."

Somehow I managed to put the towels on the chair before escaping from my embarrassment.

"HE was in the bath. You never said that he was in the bath," I hurled at Mrs. Parrot accusingly.

"Did you give him his towels?"

"Yes. But you never tole me that he was in there."

"Does it matter?" She was all laughter and reassurance. "He didn't mind who took up the towels. He needed them to dry on and was expecting someone to bring them."

I was not convinced that he didn't mind my invasion of his privacy.

Later, back on the seat by the butt, Goody, Runci and I sit cracking a handful of freshly gathered hazelnuts. A welcoming shout goes up as John Strachey strides around the corner with the boys in tow. I go cold. Will he see me? Will he really have minded? The game begins. He grabs randomly from the jumping throng of bodies. He swings each captive in circles, by their arms. Watching, hiding behind everyone, I'm suddenly grabbed by the hand.

"Why, hello, it's you, green shirt. Thanks for my towels." I am hurtled around in weightless joy. He didn't mind.

After the game we go for some more nuts. Cracking the shells with our teeth and eating the nuts one by one is a slow process. The wait between eating each little crunchy, creamy reward is too long.

"Hey, Goody. We should collect lots, crack them all first and then eat them."

"That's a good idea, but what can we put them in?"

"I expect Miss Bailey would give us a pot or something. Let's go an ask."

"You can borrow two of my big jam jars," she said, "But be very careful with them because they're glass. And let me have them back after."

We gathered a full jar each quite quickly. The nuts were very plentiful that year. Cracking all the nuts took a lot longer. It was hard on the teeth and required a lot of self-control not to eat them. At last we finished. We threw the shells into the wood before sitting to eat the nuts.

"This was a good idea. They're yummy," Goody commented with her mouth full. "You really get the taste this way."

"We can do it again tomorrow. Shall we?"

But the next day neither of us was very keen on nuts. We both had severe, unmistakably nutty, diarrhoea.

CHAPTER
FIFTEEN

We all had medical check ups. These were done in Giggy's library. We were found to be digustingly healthy until the day the tonsils were discovered.

"Say AH."

"Ahhh."

"Well, now. They really are whoppers."

Over my head I can hear the doctor saying how enormous something is in my throat. That it is urgent to have them out. My throat is sore, and I do keep wanting to swallow something lumpy in it, but what do they mean by have them out. I have to say "Ahh" again, so Mrs. Samuel can look.

"Don't worry, Ann," she says soothingly, "The doctor will make your throat feel better."

"Yes, Ann," the doctor confirms, "It is nothing at all to worry about. You will go to sleep in the hospital and when you wake up your tonsils will be gone."

I'm given the usual bribery about lovely ice cream and jelly to soothe a little soreness which will soon pass, and the confidence trick works superbly.

In Guildford Hospital I am in a bed in the middle of a long row which stretches the length of the longest room I've ever seen. On either side, my fellow patients are soldiers. In a few moments we are bosom pals. We exchange confidences. They reassure me there's nothing at all to having tonsils out. By now I'm getting very hungry so I ask about mealtimes.

"Nurse. When can I have something to eat?"

"Not until you've had those tonsils done. Then you can have some lovely jelly and ice cream. It won't be long. Go to sleep now."

"But I'm so hungry, I can't go to sleep," I complain to one of my new friends. He is sympathetic.

"I've got a sweet bar you can have, if you promise to put it under your pillow. You mustn't eat it now before they do you or you'll be horribly sick. You can eat it when you wake up. Keep it for when you feel better."

I promise. It's a special secret between us. I hide the bar quickly under my pillow. The thought of it soothes me. I fall asleep.

I wake up briefly in the dark. I wonder how much longer it will be before my tonsils are done. My throat is very sore. I wake again as the grey light of dawn begins to return the lost colours of the night. I am very hungry. I reach under my pillow. The sweet is still there. I can't resist the temptation to taste it. Furtively removing the wrapping, I bite off very small pieces, munching, savouring each morsel. It is a crunchy toffee nutty confection. It is delicious, but it hurts terribly to swallow. The pain can't overcome the irresistible urge to eat it. The sickness, when it comes, is frighteningly red.

We receive a severe telling off. The nurse in uncrumpled stiffness is tall and cross.

144

"You should have known that it would harm her throat. What a stupid thing to give to a child," she reprimands my friend.

"I was hungry," I try to defend him, "He gave it to me because I was hungry. He gave it to me to eat when I felt better."

"You should never have eaten it without asking," she chides. "You knew that we were going to give you something more suitable this morning."

She obviously doesn't understand how hungry I was.

Later, in a playroom, there are new friendships to be made and toys to amuse. One happy little boy teaches us all the verses of his favourite song: "O Canada, My Home and Native Land". When we tire of that, we learn "The Petals of the Daisies". Our throats heal quickly. We check how they look in a mirror. We compare with each other. Mine looks different to the others. My uvula is pulled to one side whereas theirs hang down in the middle. I blame it on the crunchy bar whilst concluding that it was worth it.

We all learnt folk songs and hymns at school. For the Guildford eight they were our "pop" music. When out with Mrs. Samuel we often sang as we walked. The hills would echo with a loudly, raucous, rendering of "Jerusalem" or "Molly Malone". But current popular songs we picked up from other children or Mrs. Parrot. If we had learnt any during our separations, we would have concerts when we got back together, to teach each other something new to sing.

Without television, radio or newspapers to awaken our curiosity, we remained both innocent and

145

unknowledgeable. Country children in those days were usually related to the farming community. They learnt about life from nature. Apart from a few cows down in the valley, the only creatures we were familiar with were Mrs. Raven's chickens, so we retained an ignorance, even to the point of disinterest, about procreation. Any reference to bodily functions was considered rude. Slang names for parts of the body were thought to be dirty words. They were used with glee, but never within earshot of an adult. When we were allowed to walk to school on our own, the boys would sometimes teach us sing-song verses to chant. Where they learnt them we had no idea. Marching down the hill we'd shout them to the empty landscape thinking they were very risqué. One of our favourites was in rhyming couplets about Nebuchadnezzar:

> Nebuchadnezzar the King of the Jews,
> Bought his wife a pair of shoes,
> When the shoes began to wear,
> Nebuchadnezzar bought . . .

and so on with the only criteria being that the line endings rhymed. At the end he sings that he's lost something in the po.

There were a spate of "Chinese Verses" which used the last word of a sentence as a beginning to the next. Certainly we girls didn't know the meanings of many of the hidden references, but that didn't stop us yelling them with bravado.

146

I took my girl to the station to see the engine
  shunt
A spark flew out of the boiler and whistled up her
Country girls are pretty, they do a lovely dance
They cock their legs right over their heads
And sit down on their
Ask no questions tell no lies
Ever see a donkey doing up his
Flies are a nuisance, dogs are worse
And that's the end of my Chinese verse.

We must have caught the usual childhood illnesses. Apart from a vague memory of being itchy, they are soon forgotten. None of us broke any bones. I did contract scarlatina. Whilst I was whisked off in an ambulance to an isolation hospital, the others were quarantined. I don't know how long they were kept away from school, but I was ill for quite a long time. I was sent to foster parents in Ottershaw for convalescence. I thought it was paradise. My foster mother was wonderful. I thought that they had prepared everything just for me. I didn't realise that they cared for children in need on a temporary basis. I was given a little bedroom of my own with shelves of toys to play with. The most joyous of these was a doll's pram. I was allowed to push the pram up and down the pavement, for their house was one in a row of houses alongside a real road. Being part of a family once more, it was the most natural thing to call my carer Mummy. She always spoke gently and carefully for my understanding.

"I'm sorry, Ann, but you won't be able to go home for a while yet. There was a fire. No-one was hurt at all. The fire was on the roof. The thatch caught alight. The hole in the thatch has now to be mended, so it will be a while before you can return."

"But I don't want to go back. I love it here with you. I love you."

"I love you too, but you can't stay here for ever."

"Why not? If you love me, and I love you, why can't I stay with you?"

"Because there will be other little girls, and boys, who will need me to look after them. You have a home to live in. Some of the children I care for have nowhere to go. I look after them until a home is found for them. You can stay until it's time for you all to go back."

"Where are all the others?"

"They're all safe somewhere until the roof is finished. You'll have to go to school here for a while now that you're better."

My new school is a proper one. It is brick built with a real playground around it. In the front playground is a square, wooden structure which looks like a well in a picture book. I line up at the side door with the children and ask one, "What's that well for?"

"Well?"

"Yes, that over there".

"That's not a well. Miss will tell you all about it. It's an unexploded bomb, and that's why we're not allowed to go in the front." I'm numb with shock. I can see it now. There is a tail bit, like the incendiary fins we found, but a giant one. I learn that it really is a bomb awaiting disposal. I'm assured that it is safe and it can't explode. The structure I had mistaken for a well is there to protect it. It is forbidden for us to go in that part of the playground. Nothing of school can enter my mind past the thick, grey, cloud of fear of the bomb. At my new home it is happiness. At school it is an expectancy of oblivion.

The arrangements for returning to Newlands Corner are made quickly, leaving little time for grief. I hug my new Mum, crying that I don't want to go. She repeats the reasons why I can't stay, and before I can mourn too long, our "family" is reunited. We all walk around the house looking for any signs of the fire. We can't see anything strange at all. We expected to be able to see an obvious repair, a new patch of thatch, but there isn't one. Miss Bailey assures us that there really was a fire. Nobody knows why. Secretly we think that there might have been an incendiary, and that they won't tell us in case we're frightened. Or perhaps it was started by a bit of glass, I suggest.

As the months pass, our abilities grow. Our offers of help are more readily accepted. Running errands, usually with messages, save the adults time as well as keeping us occupied. When there isn't a reply to take back we pester for jobs wherever we've been sent. Whilst up at the Ravens' house, we ask if the hens need feeding or the eggs need collecting. At Mrs. Parrot's we sometimes help to weed her garden.

Goody, Runci and I are given a special task. We are to take a letter down to Clandon Farm. We have never been so far on our own before. We set off down the steps into the woodland, full of our own importance. The lower woodland is coppiced. Amongst the thinned out hazel bushes are neat stacks of cut branches ready for collection. There is no-one working today. The woods are silent. When we get to the stile we can see that the white scar, left by the land mine, still mars the brown, ploughed earth of the field. We clamber over, eager to complete our mission, and run all the way to the farmhouse door. A quietness hangs sleepily over the farm. Goody knocks. The knock echoes hollowly, disturbing the emptiness. Doubtful, and unsure of what to do, Runci knocks louder. We decide that they must have gone away for the day, that they're sure to come back and that we should leave the letter. Runci puts it into the green painted letterbox beside the door.

Back in the dappled light of the nutwood, halfway to the junction with the path up to the house, we find our way blocked by a soldier. We had been so busy chatting that it was as if he'd appeared by magic.

"Don't be frightened," he said. "I won't hurt you."

We were not frightened. In our innocence and trust, we had no cause for fear. Even when he took hold of our hands, pulling us from the path into the trees, I felt no fear. He now held my forearm with one hand and Runci's hand with the other. Goody managed to slip from his grasp and ran off.

"I won't hurt you," he repeated, "You have just got to touch it." His expression was stern but not threatening. His face was ruddy, with a weathered look. He had ginger hair. He nodded, indicating downwards. Only then did we notice what we knew then as a willie, his penis, poking through undone khaki buttons. Runci was nearest to it, but she looked uncomprehendingly at him.

"Stroke it," he ordered, pulling her hand and moving it onto himself. The soldier rubbed himself with Runci's hand until a funny cream dropped from the end of his willie. He looked very sad as he let go of us, moving back quickly, silently into the woods. It all happened extremely fast. On the instant that we are free, we run, not stopping, until we bump into Mrs. Bailey at the top of the steps. Behind her the whole household seems to be waiting for us. We are taken into the playroom. The room is darkened with people. Each of us has to relate our version of exactly what happened. We have to answer questions, which are fired at us so fast we can't think. Above our heads rolls the deep mumble of their discussion, not intended for little ears. The result is to hear disembodied meaningless key words very clearly.

"Soldier; camp; caught; Police; deserter; hunt; bastard; murdered; gun."

I worked out that they wanted to catch the soldier because he'd run away. I supposed he'd try to live on nuts and berries. I remembered how sad he'd looked. I didn't like the idea of being hunted with guns.

There is nothing more we can say, or do, so we are sent out to play in the horseshoe. The others are already there playing, so we join in happily. The incident lay, completely forgotten, amongst the pieces which would simply meld in the mind into knowledge in due time.

Only one innocuous incident caused me any problem later on. The group of boys at school who were always upsetting the girls suddenly became interested in genitalia. One morning I was pulled from the path by Arthur and his gang, who had been lurking in the shrubbery.

"Come on, Cab. You're a good sport. We want to have a quick look. You know!"

"Look at what?"

"Just pull down your knickers and let's have a quick look."

"No, I won't."

"Aw. Come on. We only want a look. You're diff'rent to us, an' we only want to see. Go on. Just a quick look."

They keep on and on pestering, pleading, urging one after another. I do have a sense of personal privacy, but as I already know that boys have their willie on the outside whilst girls have theirs inside, the matter is of no importance or special interest to me. Their continual appeals finally exhaust my patience. It also occurs to me that, if I comply, they might choose someone else to annoy at playtimes.

"Okay. A quick peep. That's all. Then you leave me alone in future."

They group in a semicircle of concentration. I perform a swift down and up of my drawers.

"Cor," they say, "Girls really haven't got one." They solemnly melt away, absorbing their new knowledge.

At the very self-conscious age of thirteen I was back in London. I had rediscovered my friend Rita. In fact we now lived in the same street since our move due to the bomb. We had become close, teenage friends. She loved to go to the local cinema whenever they were showing a horror film, and always persuaded me to go with her. Not only did I hate the films, they scared me witless, but to my discomfort, she thought they were hilarious. We sat together in the darkness but were poles apart. I trembled with fear, living each horrific moment, whilst she laughed. Her laughter was in proportion to the horror. She became virtually hysterical with mirth at the very worst parts. The werewolf, who could only be killed by a silver bullet, drooled blood in glorious black and white. He was hairily bursting out of his skin yet again when I received a tap on my shoulder. I turned to see three unknown boys sitting behind us.

"You're Cab, aren't you? Know you anywhere. Remember when we were at school at Cook's Place? You pulled your knickers down for us." The film paled into insignificance. Trapped in a horror beyond belief, I took the only way out.

"No. You must have made a mistake. I'm not Cab."

"Yes, you are. Ole Ann Savage, and you took down . . ."

"No, I certainly did not. Leave me alone. It must have been someone else."

Perhaps my denial made them uncertain. They didn't pursue the matter. The film demanded their attention, Rita was convulsed with laughter, I was anguished. When the end came, I begged her, "Quick. Let's go now. This is where we came in, and we've got to get home."

Rita didn't argue. We rushed out into the evening, leaving my embarrassing unwanted ghosts behind. I never saw them again. Even a small area of London is a blessedly large place.

CHAPTER
SIXTEEN

We are not really aware of how much we have changed in three years, but we are no longer at a loss to know what to do. Both Brian and Ralph are soon to sit their scholarship examinations. They are studying hard. We all have some homework to do now. Education has had a positive influence on each one of us. I love to read. Once into a story, perched on a playroom windowsill, I'm happy to be left alone. As nothing penetrates the concentration of a totally involved reader, and my attention is difficult to attract, I'm usually left undisturbed.

We have also gained various skills. All the girls at school have sewing lessons. Mrs. Samuel has taught us to knit and darn. The darning isn't a favourite occupation and our socks seem to get holes daily. We each have a "mushroom" which is made of wood. This is put inside the sock beneath the hole to give a firm surface on which to weave wool to fill up the hole.

Runci knitted. She progressed slowly from the tangles of dropped stitches and irregular shapes with a perseverance which we didn't share. She was determined to knit a scarf. Once competent enough to do so, she clicked away at her task. Our admiration grew the longer the scarf grew.

The boys built models from wood or Meccano. Tongues held between teeth in total concentration, they co-operated to fix wayward nuts and bolts in the more difficult places. Their models required much ingenuity and consultation. Large, working models took them hours to construct.

Cards became another favourite pastime. The pack we played with was unusual. The suits were coloured on a black background. Hearts were red, Clubs were green, Diamonds were yellow and Spades were white. It made identification very easy. We also painted and drew pictures, played noughts and crosses and boxes, and wrote letters more often than before. So, as we became more constructive and less destructive, the urge to be out waned. When we are usefully employed we may remain indoors.

Goody has one task she is made to do which she hates. Her father has determined that she should write perfectly. To this end, he supplies copy-writing exercise books in immaculate copperplate script. Not only does he expect to receive the completed books back regularly, but no sooner has she thankfully finished one, another arrives to take its place. I watch her suffering, jealous of her book. I can't understand why she makes such a fuss. I keep urging her, "Please, Goody, let me do some. I'd love to do it for you, honest I would."

"No. I've got to do it. My Dad says I've got to."

"But how would he know if I did some of it for you? The writing's got to be the same as the book, so how could he tell?"

She resists my pleading until she reaches a particularly awful section of *g* and *y*, which have to sit neatly on a line.

"Aw, go on then. You can have a go, but mind you do it properly."

I am in my element. I love to feel the flow of the letters curling from the end of my pencil. It is another form of drawing but structured to demand perfection. She has great difficulty in getting me to stop.

"What you've done is okay," she admits grudgingly, "But you can't do any more now."

"Can I do some more another time then?" I beg. "If I stop now, will you let me have another go?"

"Yes, but I'm only s'posed to do two pages a day, so you musn't do too much."

If left, I would gladly complete the whole book. On the promise that I can do some more tomorrow, I give her back the pencil. We forge an agreeable working relationship. She does one or two letters. I complete the exercise. It isn't long before we get caught by Mrs. Samuel.

"Joan. You are supposed to do the book by yourself. Your father wants you to learn to do good handwriting. Yours won't improve if you let Ann do it for you!"

"But I like doing it and she doesn't," I complain.

"Well, why don't you do the writing on a piece of paper while Joan works in the book?"

The idea works quite well. Whether my enjoyment stimulates Goody to have more enthusiasm, or whether it is just because we are together, her daily chore becomes a pleasant task. We both owe a debt to her father for the clarity of our handwriting.

During the holidays, on one day a week we now lunched out. This gave Miss Bailey a rest. Civic restaurants were established to serve food to those unable to cook for themselves, like a "meals without wheels". Our local restaurant was in Merrow. The village hall had been taken over to serve this purpose. It was a long, rectangular building with a porch-covered doorway at the side. We went in at the side and out at the front through the "push bar to open" type of double doors. Inside the hall trestle tables and chairs were set out to accommodate groups of four. No-one minded if you rearranged the seating to suit yourselves.

As we became regulars, a table was already set for our arrival. The food was never as nice as Miss Bailey's cooking. The meat of the day was hidden under a pile of much disliked soggy cabbage. The puddings varied. Sponge or tart was considered lovely. Tapioca, with a central dollop of red jam, instilled a growing loathing each time we had it. We stirred it violently until it became uniformly pink. This only delayed the eating. It neither benefited taste or texture. We really dreaded the occasions when they served a porridge substance. Porridge, we knew, should be creamy-white. This was grey and littered with chips of green apple peel. Our spoons became stuck with this slimy concoction so that it was as reluctant to leave the spoon as we were to eat it. At least our united abhorrence to it protected us from having to eat it all up. We were allowed to leave it if we ate some.

We never seemed to anticipate the worst as we set out for Merrow, or wonder what we would have for dinner. There were too many distractions. We usually took the private path which led from our driveway to the big hotel. From there we could reach the main road by walking down the hotel drive. It saved a long detour. At the top of Newlands Corner, the Merrow Road forked away from the road, where it began the steep descent down to Clandon, keeping straight along the summit of the Downs. This narrow uninhabited road seemed endless. On the left hand side bracken grew, so tall as to make a forest for us to play in. We ran through the tunnels our feet had trodden over time, playing hide and seek in the softly, glowing green. On hot days we welcomed the shade of it and the pungent scent. Further on, where gorse bushes resisted the spread of the bracken, we were forced back onto the road until it too thinned before the open expanse of the golf course. Here the soft mown grass spread out invitingly on either side. Finally the road squeezed between flint walls, bounding the little Merrow Church and its graveyard to emerge into the wide High Street of Merrow village. Only at this point did the prospect of food beckon to us from the hall which was across the road. Usually, after our meal, we returned by way of the golf course. At its farthest point, open downland sloped down to meet the Clandon Road. We descended opposite the turning where the long, steep driveway began an upward curve past Peggy's house.

On rare treats we went to the cinema after our meal. Mostly we walked the pavement into Guildford. Sometimes we returned to the golf course, walking behind the houses and over Merrow Down which reached nearly into the top of Guildford town. On one occasion, travelling this country route, we found that our way was restricted by a high wire compound which left just a narrow path for us to walk in single file. Inside the compound were hundreds of men. As they saw us approaching they came to the wire smiling, waving, and calling out to us delightedly.

"Rhubarb, rhubarb, bambino," they shouted, obviously friendly. Obviously not speaking our language, they still conveyed their pleasure at seeing us so clearly, that our response was automatic.

"Hello. Hello," we replied cheerily as Mrs. Samuel urged us to go past quickly.

"They're Eyeties," stated Brian. "They're our prisoners."

"What's Eyeties?" we wanted to know.

"They are Italians. Men from Italy." Mrs. Samuel decided to explain so that we didn't misunderstand. "They were Italian soldiers who were captured by our soldiers. They are being kept here until the end of the war when they will be sent back to their homes again. Now, come on, everyone. Hurry up or we'll be late for the picture."

"What did they do to be prisoners?" I asked Brian quietly.

"They was soldiers on Jerry's side, stupid. They was fightin' us, so we caught 'em and shut 'em up so's they can't escape. All soldiers who get caught are put into prisoner camps."

"They looked too nice to fight. They looked kind and friendly."

"Well, I expect they'd rather be here than fightin' the war," Brian said philosophically.

We never went past the camp again.

The big Odeon cinema was built at the top of Guildford High Street, which was the part of town nearest to us. We were always bubbling with excitement as we reached the marble steps leading into the foyer. I can only remember four of the films we saw. Both *Bambi* and *Dumbo* were a delight. The sad parts were soon brightened by their happy endings, but *Snow White* left a residue of fear. The face of the wicked Queen stayed imprinted in the mind to return at night.

On one occasion there was a second feature. The film was American. It was the sort of story which children can only partially follow, often greeted with whistles and boos. I was concentrating hard. The man and woman in the film had some deep sadness. It seemed that he was going to die. They wept as they hugged each other. They were saying goodbye when the scene changed to shots of a demolition gang. A skyscraper was being knocked down. There was a gigantic crane which had a massive steel ball, hanging from its jib on a heavy chain. The ball was being swung repeatedly at the building, which crumpled impressively.

"Come on. We have to go now or we'll miss the bus." Missing the bus was unthinkable. We could never walk home after walking all the way there.

"Oh. Can't we just watch this bit?"

"No. Quickly now. Come on."

I followed reluctantly, watching the screen over my shoulder. The ball swung again, there was a loud crack, the chain snapped and the ball began to roll along the street. There were people and cars in the path of this rolling terror. Deep rumblings overlaid with screams suddenly stopped as I was dragged out through the auditorium doors and pulled protestingly into the evening sunlight.

"What happened next? Did the ball kill the people? Did it knock all the skyscrapers down?"

"I don't know."

"But I want to know what happened."

"Look. It's only a film. A made-up story. It didn't really happen, so no-one was hurt," Mrs. Samuel sounds impatient, "Here comes the bus. We're just in time."

The bus, the low, green coach which served the rural areas, is very crowded. We all have to stand until we reach Merrow, but it's still better than walking. We chatter about the films all the way home, recalling and reliving them in detail. Today I'm the only one concerned about the second feature. The boys make up imaginary endings which are horrible. I see the steel ball in my dreams. I can't lose the worry of it.

CHAPTER
SEVENTEEN

The eldest children have left to go to their new schools. Goody, Runci, Peter and Fitz are now with me in Miss Hall's class, and I've moved up to the top group. A new girl has arrived who is in this top age group. Miss Hall suggests that that I look after her and make her welcome. This is both a proud responsibility, and a pleasure as Blanche and I have an immediate liking for one another. I've grown gawky, much taller than my peers. Blanche makes me feel smaller. Having someone my own height deceives my judgement of size. She has long black hair fringed across a wide brow. Her friendly frank blue eyes, set in a pale oval face, have that untroubled gaze which gives her an aura of self-confidence. Her questions are logical, my answers are practical. By midday Blanche has become part of our community. Her friendship is to change my personality completely. She teaches me to draw upon my own inner reserves of strength, which serves me well in the years to come.

Arthur chooses his moment to enact his spider routine with care. Pouncing out at us from the shrubbery with his captive creature of torture at the ready, he is hoping to destroy two timorous females at one go. Blanche and I are suddenly confronted by a fat hairy spider held between the grubby fingers of my archenemy. With a terrified scream I hurtle towards the sanctuary of the gazebo, expecting to be accompanied by Blanche. Realizing that I am alone, I turn around when she calls out, "What are you doing? Come back here." Blanche is standing more or less where I left her, and Arthur has vanished. I return to her very sheepishly.

"You're not scared of spiders, are you?" she eyes me with incredulity. I feel ashamed but can't lie under her thoughtful gaze.

"Well. Yes. You see Arthur's always chasing us with really big ones. He says he'll put them down our necks. Ugh, can you imagine that one crawling down your back?"

"Listen. You mustn't let him get the better of you. First, he won't have any fun at all if you don't let him see that you're frightened, and second, he'll leave you alone if you face up to him. I told him to push off. He looked a bit surprised and wandered off."

"Didn't he try to put it on you?" I stare at her with astonished respect. "Weren't you scared at all?"

"Oh, I used to be, but not any more. I found a little one on my arm one day, so I decided to keep still to see what it would do. It tickled, that's all. My old teacher said that they're harmless, even the big ones. I learnt a lot about them, and then I dared to pick up a big one. It wasn't awful at all. I'm not frightened of boys either. I'm bigger than them. They won't touch me."

164

"I wish I was brave like you, Blanche. Arthur and his gang often pick on me."

"We'll have to do something about that." She speaks with determination. "But we'll start teaching you about spiders first."

Her lesson begins sooner than I'd expected. As we stroll past the spindle tree, Blanche stops and breathes softly,

"Look. On the tree. There's a lovely little fellow."

A chunky spider, no more than a pea in circumference, is on the trunk. "Now, really look at it," I'm instructed. "Watch how it moves." It doesn't seem to be in a hurry to go anywhere. It moves upwards, then stops. The longer I look at it, the less concerned I feel.

"If you were to put your hand on the tree above it, it would just walk over the top if I frightened it."

If Blanche isn't worried about Arthur, surely I can let a small spider run over my hand. I place my hand firmly against the bark. Blanche taps lightly below, and around, the spider. I can see that the spider is petrified. It doesn't know what to do. Suddenly it goes the only possible way, running up over my hand into the safety of the branches. I let the air escape slowly from my tensed body.

"Do you see what I mean?"

I agree, in relief, knowing that I need to think about it.

Our friendship deepens into one of loyalty and trust. We sit together in class. Miss Hall keeps the double desks arranged in three rows, with aisles between.

Blanche and I have the middle desk of the middle row. The desk has a bench seat, but the desk lids, hinged below a groove designed to hold a pen, lift up individually. Under the lid is a roomy box in which we keep all our exercise books. We now use nibbed pens instead of pencils, all the time. The ink, in china pots set into the right-hand top corner of the desks, is kept topped up from a large bottle. Each week, an ink monitor is chosen to be responsible to do it. Our nibs often get broken, mainly because we try to bend them so that they produce a finer line.

For most of us schoolwork was exciting. It had become more interesting, more meaningful, and so more enjoyable. As our confidence grew in the skills we had learnt, so the challenges of the difficult, and new, subjects were tackled enthusiastically. I loved arithmetic, English, writing and painting. In primary school, learning was a pleasure keenly savoured. Secondary education managed to destroy that.

Miss Hall was teaching us about the differing forms of correspondence which needed to be written in a correct and appropriate style. We wrote business letters, letters of enquiry and complaint, as well as personal ones. One day we were set to exchange letters of introduction about ourselves with the person in the next row. A boy named Henry sat across the aisle. He was quiet and gentle. We had no curiosity or interest in one another until this exercise forced us to write to each other. I wrote about our home, our daily routine and our surroundings. He did the same. The differences in our lives revealed by these letters were fascinating.

Henry was billeted with a farmer and his wife quite close to school. The cows in the field that we passed every day were theirs. He loved to help with all aspects of farming, especially milking the cows and working in the dairy. He was determined to become a farmer.

At playtime, after we'd all exchanged and discussed our letters in class, Henry and I sought each other's company. We both wanted to learn more than the knowledge gained too briefly in our letters. I had always circumnavigated cows. Henry said they were wonderful creatures, and perhaps I would like to visit the farm to find out for myself. His love and enthusiasm for an aspect of rural life which I had been ignoring glowed in him as he spoke. He captured my curiosity. Similarly, my way of life intrigued Henry. He wanted to see Harrow Hill Copse amid its untamed setting. So we agreed to ask at our respective homes whether we could invite a friend to tea.

My invitation to Henry was arranged first. He was to walk back with us after school. We walked together, passing his cows on the way. He pointed out a Daisy there and a Buttercup here, promising that I would soon know each one, and maybe learn to milk them. Up the hill, my territory was completely new to him. Our cross country route was uniquely ours, the house, so far from public ways, retaining its privacy. Henry showed such pleasure at my "guided tour", I decided I would take him to see our hidden meadow after tea. It had become a special place for me, always giving delight at its unexpectedness. I took him to the topmost corner of the field, through the dark tunnel of trees and

167

out into the surprise of the huge wood-bounded meadowland. His reaction was just as I'd hoped. We ran into the sunlit sweetness, surrounded by multicoloured wild flowers, butterflies and bee hum. We sat amongst daisies, meadowsweet, buttercups and clover confiding our histories. Henry knew "The Petals of the Daisies", so we sang,

> Does she love me? Yes or no,
> Cos the petals of the daisies told me so.

And we pulled off daisy petals, one by one, as we sang. We kissed, vowing our love newly dawned and, worried that Henry might miss the bus home, hurried back holding hands. I felt so radiant, so benign.

School was not the place to admit such a delicate and beautiful emotion. At school we kept a low profile, preferring to write notes as our main communication. Henry wrote that I could visit the farm for tea in two weeks' time and that he loved me. I wrote about the current happenings and that I loved him. Our idyll was so brief.

Miss Hall went out of the classroom, leaving us busily working out arithmetical problems. It was the ideal opportunity to pass across the note which was in my pocket. Arthur sat behind Henry. He was being a nuisance in Miss Hall's absence, flicking paper pellets with his ruler. As I passed my note to Henry, Arthur snatched it as swiftly as a snake strikes. Crowing with glee, he leapt to his feet and began to shout to the world my private words. As he intoned our secret,

168

Henry didn't move. I realised that he wasn't going to move. My strength, born of persecution, defensiveness and the influence of Blanche, seared through my muscles and I charged at the astounded Arthur. He was no match for me in either size or strength. He went down like a ninepin with the force of my attack. Sitting astride his chest, my knees pinning his arms to the floor, I grabbed a large handful of his hair, using it to jerk his head so that it banged rhythmically on the wooden floorboards.

"Go on, Ann," Blanche yelled encouragement. "Now you know you're stronger. Let him have it."

Arthur owed his survival to the return of Miss Hall.

"Get up at once, Ann," she ordered. "You too, Arthur. Both of you go and sit down. No. I don't want to hear about it. I will not have behaviour like that in my class. You will both stay behind after school and I will deal with you both then. I will arrange to notify your homes."

I was shocked at my own conduct, yet deeply satisfied. I felt no concern about being punished, for whatever it was to be, I knew that it was a small price to pay for having earned freedom from harassment. Never again would I be cowed by the boys, and they knew that. The look on their faces confirmed it. Indeed, after an initial period of unease, we all settled to an amicable equality.

There is always a down side to triumph. I lost the love of Henry. He ceased to communicate, slipping back into his quiet shell. Tea was never mentioned again. I never learned to love cows.

After school, some message having been sent home, Arthur and I remain to explain our behaviour to Miss Hall. She listens to each of us in turn and, with what I thought was a twinkle in her eyes, says, "Well, you seem to have settled the matter between yourselves, so I think that you should now apologise to one another and start to behave like reasonable people. Brawling is no way to resolve problems. I shall expect you both to set a good example from now on by working sensibly. The examinations are not so far away. You can both sit down and complete the next exercise in your English book."

Arthur and I dutifully say sorry to each other before beginning our set task.

"Right," Miss Hall's voice breaks into the silence of our concentration, "You may stop now. Arthur, you haven't far to go, but you must catch the bus home, Ann. There's one due in ten minutes. I will give you the fare."

Arthur leaves hastily. Before Miss Hall hands me the money, she says, "By the way, Ann, your grandmother wants you to sit an extra exam. She will explain all about it. I just want to say that you don't need to worry about it. You will have two papers to do and you should pass them easily if you work hard. I am pleased with your work. Try not to have any more arguments like today's."

"Thank you, Miss Hall. I won't fight again and I'll try hard."

"That's good. Now run along. You should be in nice time to catch the bus. Goodnight, Ann."

170

As I run to the bus stop it begins to rain. Unprepared, I get miserably wet waiting beside the stop pole. It is firmly embedded in the most unprotected stretch of pavement in Surrey. There is no traffic. Anything on the road, apart from the occasional bus, is very rare. The only noise is the splattering of the rain until the sound of an engine and the hiss of wheels on water heralds the bus. Only it is not the bus which comes into view. It is a large, very shiny, black limousine. It pulls up at the kerb, the door opens and a man asks, "Would you like a lift up the hill?"

"No, thank you. I have to catch the next bus."

"It's all right, girly. You're one of the kids up at the Copse, aren't you? Your Miss Bailey knows me. It'll be all right for you to have a lift with us and you're getting very wet."

Now I notice that there are two men in the front of the car, and that the driver is nodding his head at me with an amused grin on his homely face.

"I'd make your seat awfully wet. But if you don't mind, I would like a lift 'cos the bus doesn't seem to be coming. Thank you."

"Come on then. You won't take up much room."

I'm lifted in to sit on the seat between them both. I notice that there are no seats in the back, that it is filled up with a sort of platform of rollers. As the car moves forward, the rollers rattle with the gentle vibration of the engine. My new acquaintance comments, "I'll bet you haven't seen a car like this before!"

"No. I haven't. It's the back that's different. What's those roller things for?"

"Well, you see, this is a very special car. It is a hearse. Do you think you can remember that word?"

"I don't know. Hearse. It's not an easy word to remember. What is a hearse for?"

"Well, as I said, it's a very special car only used on special occasions. People only get one ride in a hearse in their lives, so you're having a very special treat indeed. You just wait till you tell them back at home that you had a ride with us. You tell them old Bill gave you a lift in his hearse," and he chuckles with amusement.

I'm completely mystified, but we have reached the big hotel where the car pulls up to let me out.

"Here's my bus fare, Mister, and thank you ever so much for the lift."

"Bless you, I don't want the money. You just tell 'em you had a ride in a hearse."

I slip quietly through the hotel grounds, repeating his words all the way until I burst in through the parlour door.

"Miss Bailey. Oh, Miss Bailey, I came home in a hearse. The man, old Bill, said that you'd know, and that I was to tell you that he gave me a ride in his hearse."

"Well, well," she laughs with her low, merry, chuckle, "So old Bill gave you a lift, did he? In the hearse. Ha, ha. Well, you've had a treat that not many people get."

"That's what he said. But what is a hearse?"

"Oh, you'll find out one day. It's a special car, that's all. Now go down to the cellar and get those wet things off. I've saved some tea for you. You can come and eat it in here."

It was years later that I found out the meaning of their remarks, and their amusement.

We are nearing what is to be our last Christmas in Guildford. I receive an airgraph. It is a sheet of paper which says "Christmas Greetings from the Eighth Army". It is from a Captain Anderson and seems to come from Egypt. He must have been there on leave, because I know my Dad is now in Italy. Later on my Dad writes to tell me that Captain Anderson is his friend and would enjoy getting a letter from me as he's told him all about me. I add his name to my mailing list, and we write to each other occasionally.

We are all trying to make some sense of the changes looming on our horizons. We don't know if the war will be over when we have to go to new schools, or where we will have to be. Brian travels to Guildford Grammar School for boys. He is kept very busy with homework. Ralph stays at his new school and we only see him in the holidays now. Fitz and Valerie have returned to their families permanently, so we are down to five, six in the holidays, and we no are no longer as adventurous as we were. Curiosity mingles with fear each time the scholarship is mentioned. It forces us to worry about the unknown, leaving little room to think about what will happen to each other.

Gran arrives with the sole intention of discussing my secondary schooling.

"I've looked at all the possibilities," she explains. "A good education gives you the best start in life.

Everything you do will be built on the foundation of the education you receive. We want the best for you. Miss Hall says you are clever enough to pass the scholarship examination. An entrance examination will be just the same."

"What school will I go to next?"

"I like the idea of the Bluecoat School. It is a boarding school, so you will live there during term time and come home for the holidays."

I bombard her with all the questions which concern me, about where it is, what it's like, how things are organised. She only has the practical answers. She tells me at length about the unusual uniform, which doesn't interest me one bit. She lists the equipment requirements and goes on about the excellence of the teaching. In fact she sells me a package deal, the price of which is an entrance exam pass.

CHAPTER
EIGHTEEN

We all work diligently. The mock exams are so easy I can't believe there isn't a catch. We seek each other's opinions before asking for confirmation that the real tests won't be harder.

Gran arrives, this time with news that I can't go to the Bluecoat School. I thought I'd been accepted, that it was all settled. I find difficulty in following her arguments that it will be better for me to go to Mayfield School at Putney. Somewhere amongst her incomprehensible reasons, I sense that expensive might be the key word. All right, if it is too much money, why doesn't she say so? What she does say, very clearly, is that I shall have yet another exam to sit.

I have to do the paper in a room on my own. It isn't very different from those we are used to. Some of the English questions are about a poem which is printed on the sheet. When I've completed the paper I go back to the poem to re-read it, to try and memorise the verses.

Softly, silently, now the moon
Walks the night in her silver shoon,

I breathe it to myself, quietly savouring the magical description the words convey and their pleasing sound. It is my first experience of the strength of poetry.

Painting began to be taken seriously too at this time. We have all enjoyed splashing about with paints as an activity. Painting books were available, and these helped us to learn to control a brush. The spark of real creativity was lit when Miss Hall decided we needed some instruction. She taught us how to mix primary colours to obtain any shade we needed. She gave us a basic knowledge of perspective and stressed the importance of thinking about the effect we wanted to achieve, to plan our compositions.

We were to receive a demonstration. Fixing paper to an easel, Miss Hall explained about colour washing. Starting with a watery blue for the sky, she worked from the top using horizontal strokes of the brush. The paint flowed evenly with each sweep, leaving a wet ridge awaiting the next application. "Now for the moorland," she said, talking us through her actions. "It will look grey-green in the distance, with hints of purple heather. As we come nearer, the colours will brighten, the landscape will be clearer."

Before our admiring eyes, her brush, dipped into the chosen colours, continued to wash across the paper always working downwards.

"Coo. That's really clever, Miss. You are a good painter!"

"Anyone can do this, with practice. It's the thinking about what you want to paint, what the background of your picture needs to be, which is important. When the paper dries, then you can paint in the things in the foreground."

Already her colour wash looked like the hills and heather of a moorland scene. Later she added trees, hedges and cows grazing in the lowland foreground. Meanwhile, we attempted, with varying success, to emulate her skill. I decided to have a sunset in my sky. I found the blurry effect, as the wash made the colours bleed, very satisfying.

Grandad once owned a shop which sold artists' materials. I'd been told that something called a depression ruined his business and his health. It was Grandad who chose and supplied my painting materials. As the years passed the quality of these improved. They came with lectures about taking care of them, but it wasn't easy. We shared our possessions. The other children were not fussy about keeping them clean. It caused many heated arguments in the early years. Miss Hall's demonstration coincided with my receiving a box of new watercolours, squirrel hair brushes and some hand-made paper. I decided to attempt a copy of the portrait of a youth which hung on our playroom wall. It was a very old picture, done in almost colourless sombre tints. He looked down, seriously, from the frame with sad, brown eyes. His dark hair tumbled onto a white frill encircling his neck. His jacket of black velvet was fastened with buttons of pearl. The whole portrait was backed with a variegated grey colour wash.

Alone in the playroom, I had permission to stay in to paint. I soon realised that the background would have to be done last, or I might get grey on the white bits. Totally absorbed, I didn't notice the visitors until I got up to check my accuracy. Mrs. Williams-Ellis and Giggy had come in to watch me.

"That's very good, Ann. Very good indeed," Mrs. Williams-Ellis praised. "You have an artist's eye for detail."

"Yes. You have done my ancestor proud," added Giggy.

Their warm encouragement wenr to my head. When the others came in, I boasted, "I'm going to be an artist when I grow up."

"I'm going to be a nurse," Runci responded, "Nurses look after people. That's what I want to do."

"I'm going to be a policeman. I've always wanted to be a policeman," Peter tried to make himself look taller, "but I've got to grow because you have to be big to be one."

We respect each other's choices as we begin to think about the future. We are growing apart, separated by new interests and experiences. The boys have been going to a club whilst we have been going to the Brownies. A Guide and Brownie pack meet at Clandon. The organisation necessitates that we share the use of a field on the same evening. I certainly don't become a devotee. In fact I find it rather boring. I go unwillingly and once there am graceless and uncooperative. Wild flower scrapbooks and tree identification might fascinate an urban child. I have teethed on their uninspiring enthusiasms. Knots seem to have some tremendous importance. You won't lose your boat, if

178

you can do a running bowline, or some such knot. There's lots of knots for boats. I can't envisage ever having anything to do with boats. There is one knot which appears to be absolutely indispensable. Nearly everybody ties granny knots, we are told with scorn. Just any old knot will not do for tying parcels. Granny knots won't hold with rope or string. For security you have to use a reef knot. That will never pull apart. I watch with unaccustomed fascination. If everyone else ties silly old granny knots, then I must learn this proper one.

"Right over left, and under. Left over right, and under."

The knot is mastered. It's just like riding a bike. You never forget how to do it.

Peggy had a bike. We all wanted to learn how to ride it. Peggy and Mrs. Samuel, with infinite patience, spent the whole of a half-term break to teach us. We used the track beside Plover's Field, because it was the only level surface available. Hardly ideal, it was both rutted and stony. In the distance, where the boundary fence of the Ravens' cottage began, the track steeply and dangerously descended the hill. To avoid any accident with a bolting bicycle, it was necessary to make a sharp right turn at this point. Here there was a dirt pathway bordered by a ditch. Our shouts of encouragement, warning, or advice reverberated over the hilltop, putting all living creatures to flight.

Our first wobbly tries on the carefully supported cycle are so tense that the very rigidity of our muscles prevent us from gaining any sense of balance. As confidence in our tutors increases, so does the relaxation of our bodies. The day I progress to actually riding the bicycle, though still firmly held from behind, is a thrilling moment indeed.

"You won't let go, will you?"

"No. I won't let go. Keep on pedalling. You're doing well."

"You promise you won't let go yet?"

"I won't let go yet. Just keep going. You can ride now." The breeze caresses my face, blowing my hair gently, as I approach the turn. "I'm doin' all right now, aren't I?" There is no reply.

"Turn the handlebars. Turn," the shouts float from the distance behind. In panic, I become taut, pulling the wheel round so hard that the bike tries to return to its owner whilst I continue into the ditch.

"You said you wouldn't let go," I throw my accusation at everyone.

"You were riding. You can ride. You rode all the way without me touching the bike. You only came off because you panicked. Now get back on and have another go."

We enjoy Peggy's bike. We ride standing up on the pedals. We ride sitting backwards on the handlebars. We try two by two. The boys master riding on one side of the bike, using only one pedal. We reach the limit of enjoyment of sharing one bicycle. We need bikes of our own now.

We are old enough to have our sense of responsibility individually tested. If we prove that we are reliable, we may go out on our own. Miss Hall has organised a new

Guide Pack which meets in Shere. I am trusted to go on the bus by myself, which makes me feel very independent. It is much more interesting, although they are also inordinately fond of knots.

In the Easter holiday of 1944 everything seems to go quiet. Goody is going to stay with Mrs. Turney and Runci is going home. I am invited to stay with Daphne, a schoolfriend. Daphne and her young sister Audrey are billeted in a large house on the furthest side of Albury Heath. Daphne and I are the same age and live about a mile apart in London, in very similar homes. Here, her billet is too far away for us to have played together. The house stood in acres of gardens, bordering the railway line from Dorking to Guildford. The owners kept horses and dogs. I never once considered Giggy from a moneyed aspect, but these people, with their possessions, gave me an impression of great riches. They were young and treated Daphne and Audrey as if they were their own children. Daphne blended into that atmosphere of quiet wealth as though she had been born to it. (Later, when she was working in a City bank, we would meet on the train to and from Mansion House. She wouldn't allow herself to become serious about her boyfriends. She was determined that she was going to marry a millionaire. She quite possibly did.)

Daphne was excited that I could stay. She lacked companionship of her own age and resented always being dogged by her little sister. For me, it was bliss to enjoy this independence and to indulge in the rôle play of superiority and privilege. We spent our time in a leisured way, behaving like ladies. We talked incessantly

181

as we strolled the grounds and moorland. The dogs were fed with cubes of meat, chopped from a large joint. I expressed surprise at the amount of meat, and was told that it wasn't on ration. The lady told me it was horse meat, that it was especially for dogs, but that it was very tasty. She told me to take a cube and see how I liked it. It was very nice. I wondered why we didn't all eat it as meat was so scarce.

We loved to wave at the trains. Each time one passed we were waiting for it, leaning over the fence at the top of the deep cutting. The approach of a train was known long before it arrived by the hollowly echoing puffs of the engine as it fought its way up the gradient. The heath adorned the hilltop like icing on a cake. Colourful narrow sandy pathways meandered through heather, gorse and broom alive with insects of all kinds. When the sunshine brought out the butterflies it created a kaleidoscope of beauty.

If there can be salad days of childhood, then the visit to Daphne that Easter was representative of them. They edged the borders of change from ingenuousness to sophistication. Exam results loomed. We could no longer ignore a beckoning future.

School life continued, much as before, but various excursions were added to our curriculum. To allay any fears about the big schools to come, we spent a day in a large secondary school in Guildford. Outings to Leith Hill and Albury Park were organised. We heard the reports that the Eighth Army had captured Rome and I worried that my Dad was safe. Two days later we listened to the reports of the D-Day landings, and we thought the war was about to be over. Then we learned of the new peril, the Rockets and Doodle Bugs, which were blowing up houses in London, and wondered if that would stop us from going home.

Our experiences were broadened even more by Mrs. Samuel. She took us out, one at a time, on a variety of excursions. The person chosen to go was taunted sarcastically as being a "favourite". It soon wore off as we each realised we were taking turns. I was taken to several sessions of adult keep-fit classes. They were most exhausting. I joined in these advanced routines, unlike the early days in the horseshoe, with an over-exuberant enthusiasm. It was a little surprising to see a roomful of ladies exercising to keep in shape, but the warmth of their welcome soon made it feel less strange. I was also taken to the big swimming pool in Guildford, which was astoundingly blue and cold. A special treat was to be taken out to tea at Mrs. Samuel's friend's house in Merrow. That was certainly a civilising influence.

During the last few weeks of our evacuation to Guildford, Peggy took me with her to the cinema, to keep her company. She was now engaged to an American serviceman whom she adored. He had gone to fight in France and she was lonely as well as worried for his safety. Her conversation returns continually to the subject of marriage, home-building and dreams for the future. Although I can't fully understand the deep emotion she is experiencing, I do sense, without defining it, that she has reached womanhood, that she has passed over a threshold I have yet to reach.

Our trips, usually on a Saturday afternoon, give an opportunity to explore the town. Guildford is so interesting. The cobbled main street, the Castle, the alleys, the market and the river are all waiting to be discovered. Window-shopping as we wander through the town leaves us short of time, and we have to dash back up the hill to get in before the film starts. It happens every time. Afterwards we buy chips. Eating the hot, crisp chips helps to warm our wait at the dark, dingy bus stop and perfects our day.

CHAPTER
NINETEEN

It is the end of the summer term. Our date of departure is set. As the day approaches we become disorientated, not sure what to do and getting in the way of the household activity our leaving is creating. The playroom has been cleared. It echoes with emptiness. The huge cupboard, the only piece of furniture remaining, looks sadly dilapidated. The green silk behind the wire trellis of the doors is torn. The hinges of one door are broken. There is nothing for us to do.

Goody, Runci and I wander, aimlessly, down to see Peggy. She too is clearing out her room. Our visit turns into an emotional experience, a farewell gathering. As she sorts through her childhood possessions in preparation for the future she is so eagerly awaiting, our own uncertainty is heightened. Peggy understands the distance we still have to travel before we are adult. We sit on her bed, watching as she delves into a pile of outgrown treasures.

"Here. You can have this, as a memory," she gives each of us a keepsake, "Don't forget us. One day, come back to tell us how you are. We'll want to know what you are all doing."

"Oh, Peggy. We hope you'll be very happy. We'll miss you so much. Yes we will come back," we all promise. Peggy gives me a small chrome bracelet. It fits perfectly. She then hands me a second bracelet made of silver.

"Here, Ann. You can wear that one now, and this one will fit you when you are older so that you will always remember me. So that you will remember all of us."

I keep them, reverently at first, and then compulsively for ever.

Goody is going to Oxshott to Mr. and Mrs. Turney, her beloved "Mum and Dad" as she calls them. Brian, Peter and Runci are all going home. Because I can't go home, it has been arranged that I am to stay with Auntie Bee in Windsor. I have secured a place at Mayfield School, Putney, but the school is moving to Woking because a land mine has demolished the top storey of their London building. I am now so utterly bemused about the organisation of my future that I leave Guildford without absorbing any details of the event. We leave haphazardly, the sorrow of our parting obliterated by a nervous excitement. Only Goody and I, in a sudden fervour of sadness and love, exchange our addresses, swearing to write to each other and to keep in touch for ever.

The Greek shipping company, which my aunt worked for, was virtually billeted in a large country mansion called Oakley Court. The staff lived in. The firm must have agreed that I could stay with her until a new place for me to stay could be found in Woking. I slept in a dormitory with all the female office staff. During the day I was free to ride someone's bicycle around the grounds or the country lanes. After office hours we would walk by the Thames, where I could swim if an adult was present. At weekends we explored Windsor, Maidenhead or Bray. In Windsor we went to see the Castle, to plays by the repertory company or to pub lunches by the river.

All too soon I was taken to live with a family in Woking. It was a disaster. I was given a room which doubled as the family's air raid shelter. In the centre was a large, square, metal table encased in wire mesh. My little camp bed was in a corner. I had to live out of my suitcase as there was no provision for my clothes. Treated as a lodger, spending most of the time in my room, I was desperately unhappy. Then my aunt, who had been doing voluntary nursing, decided to go to India as a V.A.D.

My new school was enjoyable. My new friends suggested that I should tell our form mistress of my problems. It was arranged that I should move into the school hostel. We were there until the summer of 1945. The winter was bitterly cold. We discovered that stone ginger-beer bottles filled with hot water were ideal to warm our beds. The little shop down the road did a roaring trade in ginger-beer. The chemist, next door, also enjoyed a boost. It sold cough and throat sweets which were not rationed. We tried lozenges, pastilles and cough candy. All were sold loose by the ounce. A new friend, Joan, and I liked the Chlorodine gums best. They were small domes of black hard gum which had a flavour similar to that of the blue bobbly sweets in Liquorice Allsorts before their ingredients were changed. We each bought two ounces of these gums one lunchtime, and surreptitiously chewed them throughout a double geography period. We got caught because we kept dozing off! Apparently they were not safe to eat in quantity as they were a sedative.

The celebrations for V.E. Day on May 8th 1945 were not very exciting. Bunting was strung between the trees and the cooks made some sandwiches and cakes. Rationing left little spare to do much with. In any case, those of us with relatives in Europe or the Far East needed to have them home before we could truly believe that the war was nearly over.

In July we returned to London. Mayfield was not re-built, but it was promised that it would be repaired safely enough for us to return there by September. In fact it remained without a top floor for the whole of our schooling. As it was the science and art rooms which had been destroyed, we wasted a lot of time walking to other schools. Art lessons were held in Putney School of Art. For Chemistry we walked down to Wandsworth Boys School. For Physics we used the laboratory in Sutherland Grove School in Southfields.

It is a miserable homecoming. Gran is at work back in the city. Only Grandad is at home during the day and he is not very well. When I meet Rita, whilst out shopping, she takes me under her wing and introduces me to her friends in the area. It helps me to adjust to life back in London. All the shops are small, selling only those items which belong to their trade. There were greengrocers, grocers, chemists, fishmongers, bakers, ironmongers, sweetshops and so on, all of which serve their customers individually and usually from behind a counter. Gran has her favourite shops, refusing to shop anywhere else. Rita's Mum shops at the Co-op. Rita can't understand why Gran won't go there. It is so much cheaper, she keeps telling me, and their products are of such high quality. Gran just snorts when I try to persuade her to go there.

"Rubbish. They sell cheap stuff which isn't as good as what we buy." She warms to her theme. "Their jam might look all right, but it hasn't got real fruit in it. They use apple pulp, dyes and wood chippings to make it look like strawberry jam."

I know this is a complete libel, that she is a dyed-in-the-wool Tory who considers the Co-operative Movement to be a wicked Labour plot and that nothing I say can alter her deep prejudice. So when I'm given lists of things we need, with precise instructions on where I'm to buy them, I shop where I'm told to.

Walking down our main street on my way to the bakers, I recognise Brian and Peter. Peter is swinging on his front gate whilst Brian is standing on the pavement. I am so surprised to see them. It has not occurred to me that I might meet old primary school friends, let alone my fellow evacuees. My delighted greeting is met with reserve. They have that absent air of watchers. We pass the time of day. They are waiting to see their father coming home. It is as if they barely remember their evacuation, as if it was merely a brief disruption to their normal life. Their eyes don't reflect any interest at our reunion. They are waiting for their Dad.

But Goody and I have kept our agreement. We write to each other regularly. She is in a proper boarding school. Whenever she comes home, we meet. She likes to visit me for Gran always welcomes her as one of the family. When I visit her, it is usually to go swimming in the pool at Hampstead which is near her flat.

Together, one holiday, we plan a trip. Excitedly we work out costs and timetables. We are going back. Almost two years have passed since leaving Guildford. We feel the need to re-establish contact with the people we loved. Bursting with anticipation, we walk up from Clandon Station to Mrs. Parrot's cottage, knowing how pleased they'll be to see us, and wondering if Peggy will still be there. The cottage is empty. The disappointment is almost unbearable.

"We should've let them know we were coming," Goody says philosophically, "But there really wasn't time. Perhaps they've gone on holiday. Couldn't we have telephoned?"

"I suppose we could have found Giggy's 'phone number," I answer dejectedly, even though I haven't any idea of how we might have done that or whether they actually have a telephone.

The big house also seems silent and forlorn. Our ring of the doorbell is answered by a total stranger. We explain our visit to her. She agrees to announce our presence to Giggy, leaving us to wait on the doorstep. We wait apprehensively. Suddenly Giggy is there to greet us, smiling with pleasure. We receive the warmest of welcomes as she ushers us into her library and urges us to sit down. Giggy wants to know about everything which has befallen us since our departure. We in turn ask about her household. We learn that Miss Bailey has retired, that Peggy has married her soldier and is now in America, that Mrs. Parrot is well, Mrs. Samuel has a little home of her own and that Giggy's own family are all well. After exhausting all the questions we have to ask of each other, we request permission to go and look at our old haunts. Giggy is very concerned about the time that our return train is due to leave, that we should not be late.

"I will lend you my little watch, then you won't forget the time and miss your transport." She leaves us for a moment, returning with a string bag. Inside the bag is a small clock. "Here's my little watch. Now you will be able to keep a check on the time. It's so easy to lose track, my dears."

We do remember to thank her, managing to contain our hilarity until safely outside.

"Little watch," mimics Goody laughingly. "I thought it'd be one to wear. Now we've got to carry this silly bag everywhere we go." We wander along the path to the oak tree and become despondent. The strawberry hill has become completely overgrown with massed brambles. The path, left untrodden, is losing its definition. We find the tree. I can now lean against the horizontal branch which once was so frightening. We contemplate how small we must have been. There is no way we can force a passage up to the tunnel leading to the meadow and doubt if the route is still passable. Back behind the house, even the broad leafy ride down to the woodland seems to have become narrow with disuse. We wander aimlessly, attempting to recall our recent history. It is a failure. We are not old enough to have developed sharp memories of things past. That only comes with age. The all-pervading sense now is of loss. So many things have changed because too many people are absent. Our time has elapsed. We return to Giggy with her clock. This time we say proper goodbyes and remember to thank her for having us.

"It was a real pleasure to see you both again." Giggy's warmth comforts us. "I do wonder how you all are, you know. Please come to see me again."

As we leave for the last time, because Mrs. Strachey moves to Wales, we wonder how there can be nothing left to mark the years of our childhood. Maybe the earth remembers the feel of our feet. Perhaps the trees are reminded of us by the wind, as it makes a faint, echoing resemblance to children's voices over the empty landscape. We notice that even the chalk pit opposite Mrs. Parrot's empty cottage has become overgrown, as we hurry to catch our train.

CHAPTER
TWENTY

London changed very little in the early post-war years. The milkman now sported an electrically driven van, but the greengrocer, coalman and rag-and-bone man all kept their horse-drawn carts. Rita's Dad owned an ancient Austin car which was the only private car in our area. He tended it lovingly, only taking it out of his rented garage behind the parade of shops, for special outings. The road belonged to us. We rode our bikes around the block, sitting on the handlebars and riding backwards, in perfect safety.

At the end of our road, the last house of the terrace had a windowless side wall beside the pavement. The wall was decorated with a line of black bricks which were exactly the height of a tennis net. It was ideal for perfecting low over the net shots. The base line was the centre of the road. Once the tenant of the house came home, practice had to stop for he got most irate at the steady thump of ball on wall.

There was nothing to keep us indoors. If not playing in the street, we were either in the park or up on Wimbledon Common. The sole indoor entertainment, for most people, was the radio.

It took many years before rationing was abolished. Food and coal were the last rationed items. It took a lot of coupons to buy clothes. Gran bought material when she could get it, making our dresses for fewer coupons and money than those ready made. The day she got a bright yellow parachute silk length she was over the moon. I walked about looking like a billowing yellow balloon the material was so weightless.

Little innovations could be wonderful. When Drene, "The Shampoo of the Stars", came on the market it changed our lives. Until then, washing the hair with the powdered Amami shampoo dissolved in water was little better than doing it in soap. Once the hair was dry, either by brushing it in front of the coal fire or in front of the gas oven, a powdery residue remained leaving the hair dull. With Drene no residue was left. The hair was silky and shiny.

The availability of home perms was bliss. Before they were invented you either curled your hair at home with rags or wire curlers, rolling the hair into knobbly lumps which were hell to sleep in, or you went to a shop. Passing the hairdressers in Southfields was enough to put you off curly hair. Ladies sat underneath huge hoods from which wires hung down. These wires were clamped to their hair with hefty clips. The resultant perms were identical. All were rows of sausage-shaped curls spaced evenly around the head with a waved bit in the front.

Laundry was a problem for flat dwellers. Gran did all the small or woollen items by hand in a bowl on the kitchen table. These were then hung on lines strung across the kitchen. She ironed with a flat iron heated on the gas ring. Gran could judge the temperature of the iron by spitting on it and seeing how quickly the spit evaporated. When nylon material became popular she often accidentally melted garments. All the large linen had to be boxed up for the laundryman, who called once a week. When Dad eventually came home he bought Gran an electric iron. This was fitted into a three-way bayonet socket attached to the central light. Gran could now iron happily with the light swinging crazily to and fro!

Most of the floor coverings were linoleum. This was kept clean by mopping with a cotton mop moistened with O'Cedar floor polish. Carpets were bought as squares. Ours in the centre of the living-room was cleaned by sprinkling it with damp tea-leaves before brushing with a stiff brush. A carpet sweeper was pushed over it for normal cleaning.

Dad did not come home until the summer of 1946. The Government had learnt the dangers of demobbing the forces all at once in the First World War. This time, men were released into "civvy street" more slowly so that the labour market would be better able to cope. Having spent some months in Austria working with the Army of Occupation, Dad moved to France to help with the organisation of demobilization. He was one of the last to come home.

My aunt returned from India full of stories about Poonah and Delhi and with an abiding respect and love for the Gurkhas. She became a "Nightingale" nurse in

St. Thomas's Hospital, where she made her home in the nurses' quarters.

When I married in 1953, we still had ration books. Everyone had to register with a grocer and a coal-merchant. We chose a grocer across the road from our rented home. Because many people could only afford margarine, and some did not use all of their allowances, an "under the counter" system began. If you were on good terms with your grocer, he would let you have extra butter, sugar and so on which he had stockpiled from the surplus left by other customers. Many commodities were sold loose. Sugar was weighed into blue paper bags, biscuits were in large square tins on display; they were sold by the pound. That always left some broken ones at the bottom of the tin which were then bagged up and sold at bargain prices.

I still washed by hand, though I did have an electric iron. Our first luxury purchase was a vacuum cleaner. It was the 1960s before we possessed a refrigerator, a washing machine, a telephone, a fitted carpet and a black and white television in that order.

Joan Goody and I keep our friendship to this day. She lives with her family in the North whilst I live in the South. We exchange visits and correspond regularly. We are the last of the Guildford eight, as far as we know. Joan says that she remembers little of those early years, but then my own recollections were encouraged during teacher training when it was necessary to remember how it felt to be a child.

I wonder how the children of today will recall their childhood fifty years from now. They seem so burdened with commercial concerns and there are so many dangers which prevent their freedom. Demands of fashion, acquisitiveness, sexual awareness and an unsafe environment all take away from them the joyous freedom from care which all young creatures need.

Today I live in countryside very similar to that of my childhood. As the seasons come and go all the scents, sights and sounds take my mind back to those years in Surrey. My gratitude, appreciation and love for all the adults, now dead, who cared for us and taught us during those most precious years is my daily companion.

Also available in ISIS Large Print:

Walking In My Sleep

Jane Chichester

Untroubled by any formal education or adult supervision, Jane fills her days with her animals, imaginary companions and the eccentric people who live or work on the farm. She observes her glamorous parents' parties with a critical eye, but they are not part of her life.

When war breaks out, this peaceful existence is shattered by the arrival of a family of female cousins who move in for the duration. They bring with them a governess and, therefore, discipline, timetables and regular meals. This enchanting book, sometimes sad and sometimes hilarious, tells how she comes to terms with an invasion, which she sees as bad as any going on across the Channel.

ISBN 0-7531-9322-1 (hb)
ISBN·0-7531-9323-X (pb)

Voices on the Green

Dorothy Cleal

Born six years after the end of the Great War, Dorothy Cleal tells of a country childhood between the wars, of hardship in the Home Counties and the sights and sounds of her early life.

From songs, tantrums and sweets from Daddy Saucepan, to balancing the books after her father loses his job, Dorothy's childhood is one of happiness and hardship.

ISBN 0-7531-9326-4 (hb)
ISBN 0-7531-9327-2 (pb)

Sing a Song of Sixpence

Hazel Wheeler

A collection of tales of life in Yorkshire during the 1920s and 1930s, which include accounts of the pandemonium caused by a fire alarm in a crowded cinema, a poor family moving house, celebrations for the coronations of George VI and Elizabeth II, ice-cream made of potatoes during the war, scarlet fever and bonfire nights.

ISBN 0-7531-9328-0 (hb)
ISBN 0-7531-9329-9 (pb)

The Silver New Nothing

Sybil Marshall

Sybil Marshall was the third child born into a fenland smallholder's family before the outbreak of the Great War. They lived in a scattered hamlet in the depths of the Huntingdonshire fens, and got their living from the rich black earth, when flood or frost did not prevent them. In such circumstances they expected little, and made the most of what they had.

This collection of stories draws on the author's deep family traditions and memories, from the events of the disastrous flood of 1912, to her aunt's intriguing lodger who is exposed as a German spy.

ISBN 0-7531-9998-X (hb)
ISBN 0-7531-9999-8 (pb)